Discover Peace And Bliss Within

You Are Meditation

SIRSHREE

You are Meditation
Discover Peace and Bliss Within

By Sirshree Tejparkhi

Copyright © Tejgyan Global Foundation
All Rights Reserved 2016

Tejgyan Global Foundation is a charitable organization
with its headquarters in Pune, India.

ISBN : 9788183227865

Published by WOW Publishings Pvt. Ltd., India

First edition published in January 2016

Firsr reprint in July 2020

Second reprint in July 2023

Printed and bound by Trinity Academy, Pune, INDIA

Copyright and publishing rights are vested exclusively with WOW Publishings Pvt. Ltd. This book is sold subject to the condition that it shall not by way of trade or otherwise, be lent, resold, hired out, or otherwise circulated without the publisher's prior written consent in any form of binding or cover other than that in which it is published and without a similar condition including this condition being imposed on the subsequent purchaser and without limiting the rights under copyright reserved above, no part of this publication may be reproduced, stored in or introduced into a retrieval system, or transmitted, in any form, or by any means, electronic, mechanical, photocopying, recording or otherwise, without the prior written permission of both the copyright owner and the above-mentioned publisher of this book. Any person who does any unauthorized act in relation to this publication may be liable to criminal prosecution and civil claims for damages.

Although the author and publisher have made every effort to ensure accuracy of content in this book, they hereby disclaim any liability to any party for any loss, damage, or disruption caused by errors or omissions, resulting from negligence, accident, or any other cause. Readers are advised to take full responsibility to exercise discretion in understanding and applying the content of this book.

To the enlightened masters,
who have benevolently bestowed mankind
with the priceless wisdom of meditation;
who have illumined the path to reach the Source;
who have taught mankind to abide in
boundless love, bliss, and unbroken peace.

Contents

Preface   7
How to Read this Book   9

SECTION I INTRODUCTION

1. Why Meditate?   13
2. Demystifying Meditation   19
3. Understanding True Meditation   27
4. Benefits of Meditation   33
5. The Inward Journey   40

SECTION II GETTING STARTED

6. The Daily Practice   51
7. The Preliminary Rituals   57
8. Attain Deeper Attunement   67
9. Roadblocks in the Journey   76
10. Distractions in the Journey   84
11. Obstacles During Meditation   89

SECTION III ADVANCING FURTHER

12. Stages in the Journey   99
13. External Training   105

14. Art of Witnessing	115
15. Witness Your Thoughts	125
16. Witness Your Emotions	135
17. The Ultimate Goal	140

APPENDICES   151-158

PREFACE

The Source is our essential nature. It is the sense of being, Consciousness, Self, Allah, or God. We mistakenly believe ourselves to be the body-mind mechanism and lead the life of a limited individual. We then experience sorrow in our life. When we meditate, however, we reach the Source within. We then experientially know who we truly are.

Meditation breaks the belief that we are an individual. As we go deeper in meditation, the meditator dissolves and nothingness alone remains. The realization dawns upon us that we are meditation. Meditation, which is our essential nature, was already there from the beginning of the journey. The more we remain in this state of peaceful bliss and pure love, the more we remain centered in our core nature. Thus, meditation is also a kind of devotion where the limited individual surrenders himself in the devotion of the Self and allows Self to function through his body-mind.

Every person is a combination of vices and virtues. By focusing on virtues, those virtues can return manifold benefits in our life. Just as we can focus on the outside, so we can focus on the inside as well. When sitting in meditation, our thoughts, feelings and body sensations can distract us. However, if we train our focus of attention, then we can focus solely on the Source, regardless of distractions. This practice helps us to access the Source even within the din and roar of the marketplace.

This book serves as a guide in the journey of meditation. It is divided into three sections with 17 chapters each.

Section I Introduction

Section II Getting Started

Section III Advancing Further

The book starts with the basics of meditation. It aims to demystify meditation by examining both its superficial and its deeper benefits. It details the preparations required for practice at the body-mind level, covers the obstacles that can arise on the way, and explains the external and internal training required to master the body and mind. It answers all the possible questions you may have related to meditation and dispel your myths. Together with the theory, every chapter includes practical exercises to ensure that understanding of the intricacies of meditation can be gained through our own experience. Thus, this book serves as a systematic guide to lead you towards the ultimate goal of meditation.

The goal of meditation is to become stabilized in the timeless state of Samadhi. If we meticulously follow all the instructions and consistently practice the practical meditations, we can experience a glimpse of the state of Samadhi for ourselves.

Nevertheless, a true and serious seeker may not be content with only a glimpse of Samadhi. He or she may want to become permanently stabilized in it. If this is your wish, it is recommended that you read through this book over and again to fully imbibe the principles, and make them part of your life. Undertake the external and internal training, elaborated in Section II, so that your body-mind becomes instrumental for experiencing the Source. Consistency is the key to success, and this is true with meditation.

Wish you a happy meditation journey! May you attain the goal of stabilization!

HOW TO READ THIS BOOK

This book is designed in such a way that the reader will receive both the knowledge and the practice of meditation. Theory and practice sessions are interwoven to achieve this goal.

At the beginning of every chapter, a quotation is given. Take a pause to contemplate on the quotation, and then proceed with further reading.

It is recommended that you read this book sequentially, from start to finish. The meditations provided ensure that a beginner can progressively reach into the depths of meditation.

In this book, the word "meditation" is used interchangeably to refer to individual exercises, for example, Sound Watching Meditation. For exercises at the highest level of consciousness, the term Self Meditation has been used.

Analogies and examples are italicized in order to emphasize their importance.

 Symbolizes the practice of meditation. When you notice this symbol, read the instructions first and then practice the meditation. You may record instructions of certain meditations in your own voice for practice.

SECTION I
INTRODUCTION

1

WHY MEDITATE?
THE NEED FOR MEDITATION

> Every work in this world is done
> with the help of the mind.
> Meditation is the only thing that
> happens when there is no mind.

Imagine that Aladdin's genie is constantly at his service. He can't remain idle for a minute. Furthermore, he warns Aladdin that if he doesn't assign him work, he will devour him. Yet, whatever work Aladdin entrusts to the genie is finished in no time. The genie helped Aladdin free himself from imprisonment by his uncle, Mustafa. But who will now free Aladdin from the relentless genie? Aladdin is losing sleep and praying for a way to manage the genie who keeps prodding him for something more to do.

Our mind is similar to this genie. It can't remain idle and without work. It constantly demands more and more activity. As a result, we end up assigning it work that we don't really need it to do. When the mind is idle, it takes up the activity of finding fault with others and engaging them in arguments. If there is no one available to be blamed, it digs into painful incidents from the past. It grieves and repents over them and the blunders involved. If not focused on the past, it employs itself in getting anxious about the future. In this way, it never remains in the present. The mind constantly vacillates between past and future. Although both remembering the past and considering the future are important, this is only to the extent that it helps us deal with the present.

The restless mind drains all our energy. We find ourselves stressed and agitated. What a pity! If our boss at the office was responsible, we could complain to him. But when it is our own mind that plays such tricks on us, we are helpless. The more we try to control our mind, the more it rebels and retaliates. But the more we obey it, the more it dominates us. When it dominates, it continually assigns us work, just like a relentless boss. We try to escape from the mind's clutches by indulging in entertainment or pursuing hobbies, but our mind endlessly bounces back to regain control.

As the mind sucks all our creative energy, we are unable to focus on work at hand. We lose our productivity. Since we are not able to meet our expectations, our anxiety and stress levels rise. This adversely affects our relationships at home and at the office. We lose confidence, which can often lead to depression. Every time impurities arise in the mind – such as boredom, ego, differentiation, fear, anger, greed, jealousy or hatred – we feel our life become more miserable. As we experience this lack of inner freedom, eventually we are likely to ask, "Is this a proper way to lead my life – swinging between joy and sorrow, success and failure? Is it ever possible to lead a life that is happy, peaceful and harmonious? If so, how can it be accomplished?"

HOW CAN WE QUIET THE MIND?

The mind becomes inactive only when we are in deep sleep. The moment we wake up in the morning, it becomes active again. Under normal circumstances, we can't force the mind to refrain from doing anything, or make it inactive when it is active. However, the mind can be quieted with the practice of meditation. In meditation, we consciously enter a state of wakeful sleep where the mind becomes inactive. This state of wakeful sleep is called Samadhi. When we are asleep, there is no sense of time. Similarly, there is no sense of time in the state of Samadhi. It is the timeless state.

Practicing the various techniques of meditation presented in this book, along with an understanding of the gross and subtler aspects of meditation, will help to quiet the mind. With consistent practice of meditation, our untamed mind becomes steadfast, obedient, unshaken, and loving. It is taught to be self- disciplined. We become the master of the mind. Like a faithful servant, it renders service only when we want it to. Otherwise, it remains still.

CAN ANYONE MEDITATE?

Yes, anyone can meditate, be they a beginner, an intermediate, or an advanced seeker. The needs of each, however, are different.

For a beginner

A beginner may be a person troubled by the number of thoughts the mind entertains and is seeking relief. The beginner wants to escape from all the distractions of the mind and be able to focus in one direction. By practicing meditation, concentration and efficiency are increased.

For an intermediate seeker

Some people think that meditation is only necessary for beginners.

They believe that people who have progressed in spirituality have no further need for meditation. However, we need to understand that as we progress in spirituality, we receive and internalize higher understanding. With this understanding, our level of consciousness rises.

However, in the midst of our busy daily life this level of consciousness drops. But our mind doesn't alert us to the need to raise our level of consciousness. Instead, it acts mechanically, according to ingrained habits and tendencies, while suggesting to us such actions are born from "spiritual knowledge." In this way, we become inadvertently trapped in a habitual way of living, as the mind distracts us from identifying the real problem within. It works so subtly that we fail to notice it.

The practice of meditation helps us in such situations. It is the remedy needed to raise our level of consciousness. Once again, we can attain a state of higher understanding. Hence, it is vital that intermediate seekers should also cultivate the habit of meditation. The habit of meditation is not just limited to the habit itself. As we observe our spiritual progress through regular practice of meditation, we come to understand its importance. We are then happy to have inculcated this habit.

For an advanced seeker

Initially, one may practice meditation to quiet the constant chatter of the mind, and to increase concentration. But the real purpose of meditation is to experience an answer to the question "Who am I?", and to know who we truly are. Consistent practice of meditation helps us to know our true nature, which is beyond the body, mind, and intellect. We come to know through our own experience the sense of being, which can also be called Consciousness, the Source, God or the Self. This is the real "I", which is beyond personal ego, and is unlimited. It is the universal "I" and an experience of complete oneness.

The purpose of human life is to fully blossom. This means opening up completely and allowing the divine plan of God to enact through our body-mind mechanism in this lifetime. Meditation helps us open up our potential. It enables us to attain a state of liberation from all the habitual tendencies and patterns of our body-mind.

Here, a natural question arises, "Do I need to renounce all my activities and sit in one place for hours, with eyes closed, like a meditating hermit?" The answer: No, you do not.

Let's dispel some of the myths related to meditation in the next chapter so that we can embark on this wondrous journey with clarity. But before that, let's practice a meditation. Read the instructions first and then practice.

EAGLE MEDITATION

The eagle is a bird that views from above and has razor-sharp vision. In the same way, this meditation is related to vision and is practiced with open eyes. Therefore, it has been called the Eagle Meditation.

1. With open eyes, ask yourself which objects of red color are present around you.

2. On opening your eyes in the morning, while going to the wash basin see which red-colored objects exist on your way. Search for at least five red objects around you.

3. Make a resolution every day to see different colors. For example, green on the second day, blue on the third day, orange on the following day, and so on.

The fact is, we stop really seeing our home and what is present in it. With this meditation you will actually start noticing the objects in your home. In this way, we can increase our power of observation. There are certainly some places where we just don't look at all, but with this practice you will be surprised to find that you start "seeing" again. It may be that when you choose less common colors, such as pink, violet or indigo, you can't spot such colors easily. This means you will need to look at your entire house carefully and meticulously. Once you have exhausted the main colors, you can continue by identifying colors of different shades.

2
DEMYSTIFYING MEDITATION
WHAT IS "NOT" MEDITATION?

Eliminating what you are not is meditation.
Awakening to what you are is meditation.
Acting as what you are not is unconsciousness.
Being and living as what you are is Supreme Consciousness.
This is possible through meditation on Supreme Consciousness.

In the hustle and bustle of life, every day is filled with challenges, targets to be met, and plans to be made for the future. By the end of the day, we feel overworked and stressed. When this continues day after day, we look forward to that vacation which can give us some solace away from the daily grind. However, even if we do manage to get a vacation, our thoughts never allow us to be fully relaxed. Thoughts of going back to the daily grind start nagging at us even before the vacation is over.

We wonder how we can be relaxed in the midst of such a hectic life. We may then be advised to practice meditation. But we feel intimidated by meditation, visualizing it to be like a monk sitting in lotus posture for hours atop a mountain. We believe meditation is meant for the recluse, not for householders.

The reality is that meditation is meant for everyone and is much easier and more accessible than most people believe. Today, people from cultures in all parts of the world and from all walks of life – be they doctors, scientists, engineers, industrialists, office workers, or celebrities, from the East and the West – make meditation an integral part of their lives.

Such people are enjoying the enormous benefits of meditation. Let's unravel some of the myths related to meditation here. Once we understand what meditation is not, we will be clear about what true meditation is, and we can then practice it.

WHAT IS "NOT" MEDITATION?

1. Meditation is not concentration.

Many people practice meditation by focusing on the breath. But this is not meditation. It is a concentration exercise. Concentration signifies focusing the mind on one particular point to the exclusion of everything else. When the mind is full of thoughts, concentration exercises can make it sharp, sensitive, and alert. It is important to understand that concentration is not the goal of meditation, but concentration can be instrumental in achieving the goal.

2. Meditation is not contemplation or reflection.

Today the word "meditation" has become commonplace and is used without an understanding of its deeper meaning. "Meditation" is frequently used synonymously with such terms as "reflection" or "contemplation." As a result, its true significance has been lost.

In contemplation, we think about a subject from all possible views. We may first think about the positive aspects of that subject and then focus on its negative aspects. Finally, we know about that subject in depth and may understand it fully. Our concentration improves in the process. But this is not meditation.

3. **Meditation is not relaxation.**

Relaxation techniques, such as Pranayam or Shavasan, help to quiet the body and mind. They prepare the body and mind for meditation. But this altered or relaxed state of mind is not meditation.

4. **Meditation is not intention, or self-control, or willpower exercises.**

The mind is continuously filled with insatiable desires. No sooner does one desire get fulfilled than another arises. By fulfilling these never ending desires, we become the slave of the mind. By following an intention, or using willpower exercises, we can hold back these desires for a limited time. Our self-control increases. Later, it depends on us whether to fulfill a desire or to give it up. Although we can master our mind briefly with such practices, this is not meditation.

5. Meditation is not attuning the body to energy.

Some people believe that attuning the body to Kundalini (spinal energy) is meditation. Yet rather than dealing with energy, meditation transcends the plane of energy. Meditation is about experiencing the essence of unmanifest existence that is beyond manifest energy.

6. **Meditation is not the techniques that are used for meditation.**

Some people believe that meditation means performing austere acts such as standing on one foot through day and night. The foot swells, but we do not shift from our position. Other people believe that meditation means penance like lying on a bed of nails, burying our body under the ground up to the neck, not taking food for prolonged periods, or performing chanting repeatedly. Yet others believe that practicing yoga is meditation.

The word "meditation" originates from spirituality. Historically, spiritual seekers in India understood the deeper aspects of meditation. They were stabilized in the supreme bliss. They practiced yoga, and performed penance and austerities, to see whether they could remain in the same blissful state even during a changed state of body. However, with the passage of time, meditation became identified with these ritualistic customs and techniques. Such practices gained in importance while the actual purpose of meditation became lost. Some people even practiced these techniques to attain mystical powers. Serious truth seekers, however, would be unable to derive such results.

7. Meditation is not escapism.

We are faced constantly with a profusion of problems that may involve relationships, health, financial issues, conflicts in our neighborhood, difficulties at work, or even issues at the national level. Many people act reactively by jumping to solutions as soon as such problems arise. If asked to meditate in the midst of such problems, they consider it an escape from reality. Yet nothing could be further from the truth. When we meditate, we are freed from the clutter of the mind. We become liberated from past beliefs that can influence our approach to present and future problems. As we delve deep into meditation, we reach the state of stillness. Our level of consciousness rises. With higher awareness, we begin to observe problems moving towards resolution on their own. This is a miracle that we need to witness.

8. Meditation is not difficult.

Some people believe that meditation is too difficult. They think that to practice meditation requires a hard struggle and a great effort. However, in meditation, we do not need to actively do anything. We just need to sit and do nothing. We only need to witness whatever is going on within, and know the knower of everything. We do not need to resist anything. Thus, meditation is effortless effort.

9. Meditation is not just for monks or the recluse.

Many people associate meditation with an image of an ageing hermit seated with closed eyes on some remote mountainside. They believe it is necessary to renounce the material world to meditate, and to progress on the spiritual path. However, the converse is true. Meditation is meant for people of all walks of life and all age groups. Everyone can meditate, be they student or businessman, householder or pensioner, man or woman, alone as an individual, or in a group. Meditation can be practiced whether we are in solitude or in the din and roar of the marketplace.

10. Meditation is not just for retired or older people.

Meditation is meant for everyone. It is universal. One can practice it straight from childhood and it will add value to life. Children find their concentration improves with the practice of meditation, and they are able to perform better in class. Teens find meditation helps them to be more focused and goal-oriented in their studies. People are relaxed and more efficient at their workplace with meditation. For the householder, meditation can help attain greater harmony in relationships.

11. Meditation does not mean sitting for hours in one place with eyes closed.

The ultimate goal of meditation is to be in a state of love, joy, and peace. This can be while we are seated or walking, sleeping or awake, with our eyes closed or open. However, to begin our meditation practice, we sit in one place, with eyes closed, for at least 20 minutes. With consistent practice, we may later sit in meditation for a longer time. But this is optional.

12. Meditation has nothing to do with "out of body experience" or astral travelling.

Astral projection (or astral travel) is an interpretation of an out-of-body experience (OBE). It assumes the existence of an "astral body" separate from the physical body and capable of travelling outside it.

However, all this happens in the realm of the mind. In meditation, both the body and the mind are transcended. Therefore, such experiences are not meditation.

13. Meditation is not about visualizing an image of God.

Visualizing involves the presence of the mind. So, seeing an image of God is in the realm of the mind. The image of God is specific to different religions. However, meditation is not related to any religion. Just as the Sun is beyond all religions, meditation is beyond the boundaries of all religions. Meditation is universal. True meditation is about experiencing the one who is knowing: the witness, the witnessed, and also the act of witnessing.

14. Meditation is not just for those who want to attain salvation.

Meditation can be practiced by each and every one of us. It is like a wish-fulfilling tree. It is up to us how we derive benefit from it. With meditation, we can derive external benefits as well as deeper, spiritual benefits like salvation. It can help us to gain health and harmony in our relationships. It can also help us, more deeply, to attain true happiness and peace, which is our innate nature.

15. Meditation is not a means to gain wealth.

Some people believe that if they meditate, they will be certain to attain wealth, get the perfect job, or pass their examinations. However, it's not so. It is important to understand that meditation will not lead to sudden riches. Unfortunately, some gurus confound people with such misconceptions. There are priests and pundits who preach techniques of increasing income in the name of spirituality. Many people pointlessly become involved with such techniques. There is nothing wrong with gaining wealth and becoming materially successful. However, meditation has nothing directly to do with this. The ability to earn wealth is different in every body-mind mechanism. Meditation may help in enhancing capacity and efficiency at work, but it is not itself a method of getting a good job, or becoming rich.

16. Meditation is not a waste of time.

Do we consider taking a shower every day to be a waste of time? Surely not. It is the same with meditation. We can consider meditation as a shower we take to cleanse our mind. It is an investment for a better present and a brighter future. It's like watering a plant every day so that steadily it will grow into a big tree. However, we should not meditate anticipating results in the future.

17. Meditation is not meant to be practiced only in the early morning.

Some people avoid taking up meditation because they believe the practice should only take place in the early morning at dawn. They are not used to waking up so early. Early morning is indeed an auspicious time for meditation. The environment is supportive because our stomach is empty and our mind is still. If we meditate at that time, we can go deeper into meditation. However, this time is not mandatory. We can practice meditation at whatever time we get up, before starting our daily activities. It can also be desirable, if possible, to meditate before retiring for the day. By now, most of the myths related to meditation should have been dispelled. With a clean slate, we can learn what true meditation is in the next chapter. But before that, let's practice a meditation. First read the instructions and then practice.

"I DON'T KNOW" MEDITATION

In "I don't know" meditation, all labels have to be put aside.

When you see any object in your house, let's say a wall clock, tell yourself, "I don't know what this is." When you see any person, even your mother, don't instantly just think that this is your mom. You should say, "I don't know who this is. Let me see who this person is." Then look at her face carefully. You will be surprised to see changes in your mother's face that you hadn't even noticed. This is because your "seeing" had stopped. You have labeled your mother "Mom", so that nothing further needs to be observed. But we have to start seeing again. Now look at a chair. Don't just say, "That's a chair." Ask yourself, "What is this thing?" Seeing in this way changes your point of view. This is called "I don't know" meditation.

After seeing every object in a room without labeling, that very room will become alive for you. Every object will appear more colorful and lively. This meditation will also end your boredom.that, let's practice a meditation. First read the instructions and then practice.

3

UNDERSTANDING TRUE MEDITATION

WHAT IS MEDITATION?

One should meditate by oneself (in solitude),
Or is "Being oneself" meditation?
Being oneself is where duality ends.
When duality ends, then who is to be called as "one"?
Then even the "one" ends.

So far, we have understood what is "not" meditation. Now we must learn what meditation is. Let's understand what true meditation is.

WHAT IS TRUE MEDITATION?

1. Meditation is our true nature.

Meditation is considered to be a process or a practice that we have to "do." However, meditation is not separate or distinct from us.

The real essence of meditation is a state of beingness; a state that exists beyond thoughts. This state of beingness is who we truly are. In other words, we are meditation (though, at first, this may sound strange). Meditation is the experience of the real Self. This may also be referred to as the Source, Consciousness, God, Allah, Christ,

Self-awareness, Self-witness, or Pure Awareness. Whatever name we use, meditation is our essential nature.

Source or Consciousness is the living, sentient principle that dwells within and around each and every living being. It is only due to the presence of Consciousness – the knowing principle – that our eyes can see, ears can hear, and tongue can taste. Consciousness enlivens the mind. Thoughts arise and perish due to the presence of Consciousness. Consciousness is equivalent to the electricity lighting a bulb. There is no use of a bulb without electricity. Similarly, the body-mind mechanism requires Consciousness to operate.

2. **Meditation is our true essence and is beyond religious beliefs.**

Being of Hindu, Muslim, Sikh, Christian, Jewish, or any other faith is not to practice religion. Religion is knowing our true nature and abiding in it. Meditation is our nature, our basic disposition. The true purpose of religion is to find our basic innate nature.

3. **Meditation is the path; meditation on the Self is the destination.**

Techniques such as focusing on the breath or on a mantra, designed to begin meditation or improve concentration, are often also called meditation. However, merely improving concentration is not the goal of meditation. Concentration will improve in the process. But these techniques simply serve as a path to true meditation. People may begin on the meditation path in order to attain Self-realization, but are often distracted on this path by so-called "mystical" powers such as improved concentration, clairvoyance, clairaudience, or premonition. As a result, they stray from the real goal. By wrongly believing such gains to be the goal, they mistake the means for the end.

Existence, beingness, is an aspect of our nature. Meditation is nothing but awareness of our existence. Whatever makes us aware of our own existence, beyond thoughts, is meditation. Anything that leads us to focus on the content of our thoughts is not meditation. Meditation uses thoughts only as a mechanism, or mirror, to reflect on our own awareness.

4. Meditation is "doing nothing."

The simple meaning of meditation is "doing nothing." It is a process in which we just need to be present, and no more. However, for many people even doing nothing seems very difficult. They ask, "How can I do nothing?" But this is like asking, "How can I fall asleep faster?" Of course, we need to do nothing to sleep other than lie down. If we try hard to sleep, it will simply elude us. In the same way, during meditation we only need to be present.

5. Meditation is a practice to unite with the Self.

Meditation is also known as a yogic practice, which means seeking a state of union. This meditation, or awareness, is necessary in every field of life. No work or activity can be done without meditation because it is essential for all life's activities. The body receives the "vibration of action" due to meditation. The instruments for all our activities are then the five senses of our body – eyes, ears, nose, tongue and skin.

In this context, the senses are not referring to the organs of perception, but rather their power of perception. The eye is not the sense. It is the eye's power of vision that is the sense. All five of these perceptive senses affect our body. Usually, when our senses are directed outwardly they become involved in external objects, and our mind's energy becomes exhausted by engaging with external matters. To overcome this, it is necessary to have some control over our senses. Meditation enables this. Through meditation, it is possible to inwardly direct the energy that is otherwise consumed in the external world. Meditation shifts the mind from external objects and stabilizes it within.

Thus, meditation serves as a double-headed arrow. When our focus is on the content of thoughts and sensual objects, it is directed outward in the external world. However, when we use these sensual objects and thoughts as a medium to know our own existence, the focus is directed inward. This helps us to unite with the Self, our true nature.

6.   Meditation is wealth itself.

Attaining the true wealth of meditation helps us to regain our high level of consciousness. This helps us to take the right decisions in life. As a result, we can always remain happy, and we can become a cause of happiness for others.

Having understood what true meditation is, let's understand the benefits of meditation in the next chapter. But first, read and practice the following meditation.

LISTENING MEDITATION

The power of listening is indeed a wonderful gift to mankind. We can use this power to improve our concentration. Everyone listens, but those who know the art of improving concentration while listening are rare. This meditation will help you to learn the art of listening and improve your concentration. Let's understand the meditation in detail.

1. Close your eyes and sit in your normal meditation posture.

2. Keeping your body steady, listen to the various sounds around you. Try to distinguish them into at least five different types of sounds.

3. If you listen to the sound of a rotating fan, then there may be various other sounds contained in that sound. Listen to them carefully. The sounds could be from the motor of the fan, the bearings of the fan, or other parts of the fan.

4. While you are seated in meditation there may be many different sounds you will be able to hear. These sounds could be conversations between people, children playing, the clattering of vessels, or vehicle sounds both near and far. There may be the sound of something falling, the sound of somebody's footsteps, or the sounds of television, radio or music playing. You may hear the chirping of birds, the barking of dogs, the noise of an argument, or the gentle sound of flowing water. Listen to all such sounds.

5. Try to identify each and every type of sound that is around you, and distinguish between them. Try to identify even the minutest of sounds.

6. When there are no sounds, then try to perceive the sound of silence. Experience the stillness.

7. You may even listen to the sounds going on within your body, such as the sound of your breathing, or the sound of your beating heart.

8. After identifying five different types of sounds, open your eyes.

9. Every week, continue to increase the number of sounds you can identify and listen to.

4
BENEFITS OF MEDITATION
GAINS IN THE EXTERNAL WORLD

Whenever you have an option to do one of the two things, always choose to do something new. For doing something old, the mind is required. For doing something new, awareness is required.

Socrates was a renowned philosopher and teacher. As one of the most original, but controversial, philosophers of ancient Greece, his teaching profoundly influenced Western ideas. At the age of 72, he was sentenced to death by the drinking of hemlock. He accepted this poison in such a way that even the poisoning became an object of his meditation. As the poison started to act on his body, first his legs stopped functioning, then gradually the paralysis rose towards his heart and head. Yet, as this process unfolded, he calmly continued to narrate his condition. He could witness his body dying, yet perceive it as a remarkable experience. The poison could not hurt Socrates within. It could not change his inner state of being, which remained unchanged.

Jesus was inflicted with many external wounds, but none of these injured him within. His inner state remained unagected by those who attacked him. One who is able to meditate on the Self cannot be injured by the wounds of the external world.

Lord Buddha meditated for six years to unravel the hidden secrets of life. Thereafter, he made that divine knowledge available to mankind so that human life can be led to peace and happiness.

The great saint Guru Nanak was immersed in meditation from his childhood. At the age of 30, he disappeared into a river and meditated there for three days. When he emerged from the river, he was an enlightened master.

People often question what they can gain through meditation. But the question should rather be what depths they wish to reach through meditation practice. Meditation can help us excel in every field of life. It can help us get rid of physiological ailments and become more productive. It can also help us attain the enlightened state like that of Socrates, Jesus, Lord Buddha, Guru Nanak, and many other untold enlightened masters. The more we understand meditation and practice it, the more benefits we will obtain. Let's explore all the merits of meditation so that we can understand its fullest benefits and our innate potential. First we will consider the benefits for our external life.

BENEFITS IN THE EXTERNAL WORLD

1. Meditation enhances decision-making power.

When we are attached to our thoughts in a particular situation, our decision-making will likely be poor. Therefore, it is important to detach ourselves prior to making decisions. With the practice of meditation, we learn the art of decision-making. With increased sensitivity, we become detached from the subtlest of thoughts and remain in the Source.

When we take decisions while abiding in the Source, we will be unaware of the future results. But when the results arise we will appreciate the perfections of such decisions. To put it in a nutshell, all our decisions should come only from the Source. As they are divine decisions, in line with the divine plan, these decisions lead to our highest potential.

2. Meditation eliminates mental lethargy.

Like those with a lazy body, there are many people with lazy minds. They avoid serious thinking. Due to mental sluggishness, they find it easier to become worried than to engage in contemplating a right course. By contemplation we get to know the essence of the deep workings of the inner psyche. It enables us to become aware of the nature and patterns of our body-mind mechanism. Meditation ends the laziness of the mind. While the average person soon tires from only a little amount of thinking, people who meditate are able to reach the depths of any subject. Meditation helps us develop the natural mind into a sharper one.

3. Meditation enhances concentration.

If we consistently practice meditation with the proper understanding, our ability to concentrate improves. Only a concentrated mind can access the depths of any subject. The ability to concentrate enables us to focus on work over longer periods of time, and it can help us to achieve all our aims in the external world.

Even when reading, a focused mind is needed. A non- meditating student finds difficulty in attending to one topic for an extended period. The mind constantly wanders, in every direction, away from the purpose of studies. In contrast, the student who meditates every day is able to concentrate and study effectively. Through concentration, memory retention and recall are also strengthened, as distraction and absent-mindedness are reduced. Meditation can help maintain tranquility amidst the noise and distractions of external life.

4. Meditation raises creativity.

The consistent practice of meditation raises our creative intuition.

Creative ideas, in fact, do not emanate from any individual person, but all in reality originate from the Source. Creative ideas simply float around us in the atmosphere. Whichever body-mind mechanism is the most receptive becomes the channel through which such ideas can flow.

It is a misunderstanding, therefore, to believe such ideas or solutions are the product of our own intellect. Creative ideas stop emerging when we claim such ideas as our own. By meditating with an understanding that – "I am merely present, I am just the medium, I am receptive to the ideas I receive" – new creative ideas will begin to transpire. Thus, meditation helps to remove the receptive blockage and enables creativity to flow. Meditation performed for years without proper understanding will not yield benefits. But meditation performed for a short time with the right understanding will yield results.

5. Meditation enhances capacity and productivity.

Without the practice of meditation, we find we easily tire after completing even short tasks. With consistent meditation practice, our willpower improves and our capacity to work is enhanced. We are able to work for longer periods of time with better productivity and quality. This can help us to be more successful in the external world.

Some of the reasons for this improved capacity are given below.

- Through daily meditation practice, concentration is enhanced and awareness is awakened. As a result, the intellect sharpens. If the nervous system is tension-free, its capacity increases and so does its efficiency.

- Daily meditation practice relaxes the body and the mind. The mind becomes calm and can reflect in new directions. Such a creative mind becomes more capable. As the mind relaxes, so also the body heals. A healthy body gives us more capacity for work.

- Viewed scientifically, it is the habit of the mind to exhaust itself by becoming engrossed in the external world. The mind tires quickly because it drains away energy. Meditation plugs this drainage of energy, and resulting fatigue, and thereby augments the body's energy reserves.

6. Meditation improves consistency.

It is common for us to take up tasks but fail to be regular in addressing them. We become easily bored, so we begin a task only to abandon it or leave it for later completion. Tasks which we eventually complete don't derive the desired satisfaction or outcome. With the daily practice of meditation, our consistency improves. This can have positive effects in all spheres of activity in which we engage. Irrespective of the external environment, we can work consistently every day and progressively increase our work duration. Consistency and persistence ensure success. It thus becomes natural to lead a life based on these values.

7. Meditation augments problem-solving ability.

In everyday life, we consistently face problems related to our body-mind mechanism and the people around us. When we try to solve these problems in a reactive way, our problems merely multiply. Meditation helps to resolve these problems in the most effective manner. Through meditation, we can look at problems in a detached fashion, and from an alternative perspective learn to decode the hidden messages that lie behind them.

When we watch a magician's show from the front, we are confused by the tricks. However, if watched from behind, we would soon understand the background preparation involved in creating the illusions that confound the audience.

Similarly, when we look at problems from the front, we find them difficult to solve. However, when we meditate, we begin to observe our thoughts from the other side. We attain the state of pure silence from which both silence and noise arise. Thereafter, we are able to witness a miracle. We see our problems being solved on their own. This is also called "Other Side Seer" or OSS. The purpose of meditation is to attain this state.

8. Meditation advances listening ability and raises sensitivity.

Meditation brings about a considerable change in our listening and sensitivity. With consistent meditation, we begin to detect those sounds which others cannot hear. We begin to perceive and understand those things which other people cannot know. We begin to understand the true depths of the mind. We become more sensitive towards our thoughts. We begin to appreciate the games and tricks the mind can play. We begin to realize how it is just our thoughts that make us happy or unhappy, angry or egoistic. Our thoughts begin to come under our control. We are able to restrain our emotions while becoming sensitive to the subtlest experiences. We can realize our mistakes, and exercise caution to not repeat them.

9. Meditation gives choice over emotions.

Most people find that they are dominated by their emotions. Ask yourself the following questions. "Am I able to control myself in minor conflicts? Can I walk away from my country's football match? Can I give away my favorite possession? After making a decision, am I willing to fulfill it? How do I behave in stressful conditions? Can I bear any problem easily? Am I able to maintain a self-restraining fast?" All this is possible through meditation. Meditation can help you choose to overcome your emotions.

Having understood the benefits of meditation in our external life, let's understand the deeper benefits of meditation in the next chapter.

MUSIC MEDITATION

1. Sit in the meditation posture and close your eyes. Join your index finger and thumb, or use any other posture of your hands that is convenient.

2. With your eyes closed, listen to the sound of a flute through your internal ears, that is, listen in your mind. Realize that actually the flute's sound is not playing outside. Just as you listen to a movie or a familiar song in your mind, listen to the sound of the flute in the same manner.

3. Listen only to the sound of the flute; if you hear the sound of another instrument or anything else, just ignore it.

4. Now open your eyes.

In this experiment, you should change the listening sound each time you sit for a meditation session. You can choose to listen not just to a flute, but later to drums, a piano, a violin, a trumpet, and so forth. Listen to a different sound every day. This will help enhance your power of concentration.

5
THE INWARD JOURNEY
DEEPER BENEFITS OF MEDITATION

*The mind becomes the
master when awareness goes to sleep.
The mind becomes a servant
when awareness, backed by
the strength of meditation,
announces itself as the master*

Meditation delivers so many initial benefits in external life that we can stop progressing further. However, the real benefits are yet to be realized and without these we can't say we have utilized meditation to its fullest potential. Let's understand the deeper benefits of meditation now.

DEEPER BENEFITS OF MEDITATION

1. Meditation develops detached enthusiasm.

The practice of meditation develops an approach of detached enthusiasm within us. It encourages us to perform actions enthusiastically without being attached to their results. We also become detached from the desire to know what the result of our actions may be.

Many people become trapped by the expectation of receiving rewards for their actions. Even while rendering selfless service, they may initially serve well but when their actions bear fruit they wish to claim the credit. To avoid such preoccupations, we should be enthusiastic in our action, but detached from the fruits of our action. By practicing meditation, we gain the power to achieve this balance.

Now think about all your activities from morning to night, and contemplate "How will my life be if I perform every action with detached enthusiasm? How will I get up in the morning? How will I eat food? How will I conduct my work? How will I offer someone help?" With detachment, you are no longer concerned by trivial matters such as not receiving thanks in return for a compliment, or an acknowledgement for providing help. Thus, you will remain detached from the fruit of your actions – such concerns will no longer bother you. With faith in the natural process that whatever is yours will come to you, and nothing will stop this, you can live your daily life with a feeling of ease and acceptance.

2. Meditation helps to witness emotions.

Generally, when we sense negative or uncomfortable feelings, we try to escape them by indulging in distractions. These might be playing music, watching TV, eating out, shopping, or simply venting our anger on somebody. If we choose food as our distraction, our bad feelings might subside but our weight increases. Many people who develop obesity are really suffering from emotional stress. Of course, it's not just obese people who have difficulty managing their feelings. For most people, there are only two ways of dealing with negative emotions: either suppress them within, or express them by shouting aloud and abusing other people.

Shouting at others serves the ego, but it does not remove the emotional stress. We still suffer the turmoil of our inner emotions.

But there is a third way of handling such emotions. With the practice of meditation we learn to witness emotions as they arise in our body. This way, we neither keep emotions within ourselves nor vent them out on others. We just observe them, as if they are not part of us. They have simply arisen in the body-mind mechanism that we use. This approach is a significant paradigm shift.

> *Imagine we are cutting thick cloth with scissors, and we hear the scissors complain: "This cloth is so thick.... It's so hard to cut.... Why make cloth so difficult?"*

Here we understand that these are the feelings of the tools we are using and are not our own. In the same way, we can observe emotions arising in our own body from the perspective of a detached witness. When we believe ourselves to be the body-mind mechanism, we identify with all that affects it. But as a detached witness we can tell ourselves, "These emotions are not in me (the real "I"). They arise in the tool that I use, the body-mind mechanism. The real "I", or Consciousness, is the knower of this mechanism. It can witness these emotions and know they are just temporary."

Meditation helps us observe these emotions from our original state of being. Just like the weather changes over time, we can watch our emotions change with time too. From morning to night, our emotions undergo change. Whenever our mood changes or we recall old memories, we give an opportunity for emotions such as grief, despair, or anguish to arise. Both our inherited genes and our childhood upbringing are a stimulus for this. With consistent observation, our entire stock of inwardly suppressed and troubling emotions can disappear. We can realize that we are not the body and that it is only an instrument for our use. Once we recognize that we are not the body, then we are no longer affected by its emotional distress. Thus, through the practice of meditation, we can free ourselves from all such suffering.

3. Meditation teaches the art of being in the present.

With the practice of meditation, we learn the art of being in the present. When we are in the present, we observe only our breathing, our listening, our eyes perceiving, and perhaps our hands at some work. We are aware of everything happening in the present, and at the same time are also aware of our beingness, our sense of presence.

The present has immense power because the mind has no role to play in it. The mind plays a role only while being in the past or future. It gets worried about the past or anxious about the future. As soon as we are in the present, the mind surrenders and only silence prevails.

> *The practice of meditation helps us with situations in our daily life. If we wish to learn a valuable lesson from the past, we quickly visit our past – just as the comic character Superman speeds around the earth in a flash. Without getting stuck in the past, we immediately return to the present. If we need to plan, or contemplate on something for the future, we quickly visit the future just as the comic character Spiderman does. Spiderman throws his web to the exact point where he wants to go. We, also, decide exactly where we want to go in the future. As soon as the purpose is served, we immediately return to the present.*

4. Meditation raises the level of awareness.

If you turn on your television in the morning, and open all windows and curtains, will you be able to see the television screen clearly? No, the screen will appear pale and the colors weak and faded. Does this mean there is a problem with the television set? No, because you can view the same television screen perfectly clearly at night. Although the screen remains the same, its clarity depends on external factors.

After practicing meditation, some people claim they can experience a clear sense of presence. Others may say that the experience is not so clear. The important point is that the experience of the Source never changes; it is only our level of awareness that changes. Awareness levels will always fluctuate, particularly if we don't contemplate and meditate regularly. But people who consistently meditate and contemplate deeply are able to maintain high levels of awareness. This should encourage us to continue with the practice of meditation and contemplation.

5. Meditation helps reveal our faults in the light of a sense of being.

It's a normal human tendency to venture into the imaginary world. We make up many stories to engage our mind in imagined thoughts. But while making up such stories, we are usually unconscious of how this thought process actually works. With the practice of meditation, our level of awareness increases. We begin to open up and understand the hidden alleys of our mind, secrets of which we were unaware begin unraveling.

In meditation, we are able to question our thoughts. We ask: "What's going on inside me? Which thoughts keep arising within me? Which stories am I inventing now?" We can witness negative thoughts we may be carrying against others, such as "This person ignores my importance… He does not respect me…. He is being unfair." At this point, we guide our mind to stop and ponder on these thoughts. We firmly tell the mind, "You are unaware of the complete picture and are focused on just a narrow view. Come out of this imaginary world and stop inventing tales." With this, the mind gradually becomes quieter. Our tangled thoughts begin to untangle. We restore the perspective of our innate untroubled nature leading to our happy natural state.

6. Meditation helps maintain complete health.

Patients are regularly recommended to take rest along with their medications. But few people really know how to rest and relax. By practicing meditation, we learn effortless relaxation, which advances restoration to health.

Complete health comprises our well-being in all physical, mental, financial, social and spiritual facets of life. As we go deeper into meditation, mental illnesses, such as anxiety, depression, stress, and mood swings, can vanish. Diseases such as asthma, high or low blood pressure, paralysis, and heart disease have been noted to improve with meditation practice.

Meditation revitalizes us physically as well as mentally. We become a powerful magnet whose power attracts only positive energy. Without meditation, those entangled in negative attitudes not only repel positivity but also invite ill-health, pain, sorrow, and many other troubles upon themselves. Meditation has proven positive effects on the total condition of our health, even though this is not its only goal.

7. Meditation offers the bliss of silence.

By practicing meditation, we begin to experience the bliss of silence. Initially, we may not understand how we can be happy in silence. We may feel that silence just produces boredom. But the bliss of silence is reached by forbearing the phase of boredom and then transcending it. The true bliss experienced in silence is not like the joy derived from worldly pleasures. It is beyond both worldly joy and sorrow.

However, to reach the state of blissful silence we need the proper attitude to meditation. If we meditate with expectation of a blissful experience, our active mind will be constantly checking whether it's experiencing bliss. This constant checking prevents us from going deeper into meditation. However, if we quietly meditate, without expectations or checking our state, gradually we enter the deep experience of Source. We then realize we can sit in that blissful state of silence for hours. When we begin observing everything from that state, we understand that no feeling or thought can touch us. We witness everything arising from silence and dissolving into it – just like the waves in an ocean. This is possible with consistent practice of meditation. We should learn to close our eyes for some time in meditation in order to keep them open for the rest of the day.

8. Meditation brings awareness of "Who I am," our original state of being.

Due to ignorance, we are caught in our own web of misconceptions and false patterns of thought. This leads to a sorrowful and unconscious life. The only way out is to awaken ourselves from this slumber. When we awaken from this unconscious state and realize our true nature, it's like a eureka effect.

The most important question of spirituality is "Who am I?" When we delve deeper into meditation, we know its answer through our own experience. We become aware of our sense of being, our essential nature, and who we truly are.

When we repeatedly ask "Who am I?" this thought becomes superior to any other thought. Thus, if something frightens us we ask, "Who is frightened?" The answer quickly comes "I am." But when we ask further "Who am I?" we can know that our true Self is independent of fear. By placing such constant self-enquiry before every thought, we realize we are no longer bothered by worry, sorrow, or pain.

Through consistent practice of meditation, the realization dawns upon us that what we truly are is love, bliss and peace in essence. Among all living beings, the unique experience of Self-realization can happen only through the human body-mind. This is the whole and sole purpose of human existence. We then surrender our separate individuality and serve as a mirror for the Self to experience and express itself. This is devotion.

Initially, the beginner is motivated to practice meditation for the sake of tangible benefits and relief from the trials that occur in life. However, when he tastes the sweet nectar of devotion, he is prepared to surrender his personal needs and abide unconditionally in the experience of nothingness. In the process, many benefits are incurred. However, the devotee is disinterested in these benefits as devotion in itself becomes the highest source of fulfillment for him.

Let's get started with the actual journey of meditation now. Let's see how we can make our surrounding environment conducive so that we can dive deeper into meditation in the next chapter.

MANTRA MEDITATION

Before this practice, we should understand what mantra meditation is. In mantra meditation, a word or sentence is continuously repeated silently in the mind. After a while, the mind becomes naturally transfixed on the word or sentence. Some people use the name of a God they believe in as a mantra. They repeat the name of this God with utmost devotion in their mind. Alternatively, we can use a word that contains a powerful vibration. One such example is the word "Aum." Some people use these powerful vibration words together with the name of God to get the benefits of both power and devotion. Such an example is repetition of the words *"Aum Namah Shivay."*

Steps of this meditation are:

1. Before meditation you may set a buzzer timed for 10 minutes.
2. Sit in a comfortable posture for meditation and close your eyes.
3. Whatever mantra you wish to repeat, silently repeat it in your mind with the feeling of love and peace.
4. Whenever the mind wanders away, bring it back and continue with repetition of the mantra in your mind.

The benefits of this meditation are immense. It not only improves concentration, but also introduces your mind to a no-mind state. You become completely immersed in devotion.

SECTION II
GETTING STARTED

6

THE DAILY PRACTICE

PREPARE THE ENVIRONMENT

> Ignorance is the disease;
> Understanding is the
> remedy. Unawareness is the
> problem; Self-awareness is
> the solution.

In order to have a good night's sleep, we prepare our environment. Some people like to take a hot bath before sleep. Others may need relaxing music to help induce slumber. We usually need to ensure we have a dark and quiet room, and perhaps the right bedding to create a soothing feeling.

If we prepare so much to achieve peaceful sleep, how much should we prepare to delve deep into meditation? As we become proficient in its practice, we become able to practice meditation anytime and anywhere. However, beginners should particularly consider environment when attuning themselves to meditation. Let's look at the factors involved to prepare the ideal environment.

PREPARE THE ENVIRONMENT

1. Time

The ideal time for meditation is around sunrise and sunset. At these times, the stomach is neither too full nor too starved. In the morning, the atmosphere is cool, fresh, and pure, which enables the mind to become relaxed, calm, and clear much faster. At this time, we are neither fully asleep nor fully awake. We are in a condition known as "alpha state," when the brain is relaxed and its frequency is low. This state is similar to the original state of our being. In the evening, after working throughout the day, we are tired and in need of rest. In this state, the brain has again returned to a low frequency.

It is essential to meditate at a particular fixed time as this helps in concentration. If we regularly perform a task at a particular time, the mind becomes programmed for that task and stops behaving haphazardly. In the beginning, to build the mind's concentration and reduce its instability, these considerations are extremely important.

2. Place

As a beginner, we need to be careful about the place where we meditate and its surroundings. Later, as we advance in the practice, we can rest in a state of meditation wherever we are seated, or even when we are on the move.

It is not essential to have a separate room for meditation. We may choose any practical room or any corner of a room. Ensure that the room is well ventilated and the environment in the room is clean, calm, and quiet. To prevent visual distractions should we happen to open our eyes during meditation, we can sit in front of a plain wall. We may also choose to meditate in natural surroundings. External nature helps in awakening our internal nature. However, we should ensure that we meditate at the same place every day.

3. The Seat

Choose a comfortable seat for meditation. We may use a cushion or a mattress, or a blanket on a hard surface. The seat should be such that we won't feel uncomfortable or tired, and will enable sitting in meditation for the appropriate time. We should ensure that the seat is used exclusively for meditation, and not otherwise associated with other things such as watching entertainment on television.

If we meditate consistently every day at the same place, on the same seat, in the same posture, at the same time, with the same technique and type of meditation, then our body will automatically become ready. We develop a habit with the meditation seat. As soon as we sit on it, our mind gets a clear indication that at that time, on that seat, we are seated only to practice meditation. Thus, our thoughts recede more easily and we can reach the depths of meditation much sooner.

4. Switch off telephones

We should ensure that cell phones and telephones don't ring during meditation. If there is such a possibility, then switch them off.

5. Peaceful surroundings

As a beginner, if we meditate at a place where people are chatting around us, then our attention will be inevitably distracted. We will not be able to meditate properly in such surroundings. Therefore, we should meditate in peaceful surroundings until our meditation practice advances. Ideally, we should choose a silent room.

6. Special environment

Beginners may also take advantage of recorded guided meditations, to get into the depths of meditation quickly.*

---

*You can download meditations for free from "U R Meditation" application available on AppStore or GooglePlay.

7. Group meditation

Practicing meditation in a group is another practical option. A group can be both supportive and inspirational as all members of the group are working towards the same goal. By meditating in a group, if meditating for a longer period, we can be motivated to do the same when alone. Furthermore, when meditating together, if a member experiences difficulty, the presence of others is a motivational reminder and can provide encouragement.

8. Seek help from a spiritual master

A living spiritual master established in the state of Self-realization can be approached to seek guidance in meditation. With such a master you will be able to share your experiences. If there is no such facility, then by setting aside your attention to physical experiences during meditation, you should continue practicing meditation regularly.

It is essential to follow above guidelines in the initial stages of meditation so that practice can continue unhindered. Let's understand the preparation required at the body level in the next chapter.

GRATITUDE MEDITATION

Gratitude plays an important role in everyone's life. Whatever we are grateful for, those things multiply in our life. In this meditation, as we pay gratitude to our body it brings about transformation in our physical and mental states. Let's understand the method of this meditation in which we become more sensitive towards our body.

1. Close your eyes for two to three minutes.
2. Look at yourself from within. Imagine your own duplicate or clone, which is exactly like you, but without sight.
3. Now witness the daily routine of your clone. Closely watch how he/she is living from morning to night. Look at the difficulties faced due to blindness and feel this experience yourself. Watch your clone living your own life.
4. While imagining this, feel all of the difficulties arising from lack of sight.
5. After you have witnessed all this, your clone can go. Now you will be filled with gratitude for not suffering such difficulties because you have the gift of sight.
6. On the second day of this meditation, imagine your clone to be deaf, and similarly perceive all his/her difficulties. After two or three minutes, end your practice and give praise for having the ability to hear.
7. This feeling of gratitude makes you sensitive and receptive. It will enable you to better understand the pains and sufferings of others.

Usually, we tend to undervalue that which is readily available to us. The same happens with our body. Every organ operating in the body is readily available for us, twenty-four hours a day. Therefore, we forget its value, utility, and ultimate importance.

As part of this meditation, when you thank your body, you will again realize the role the body is playing and how important that role is. Then you will begin to feel more grateful to the people around you and the objects and situations you encounter in life. This meditation awakens a sense of surrender and gratitude within, which is a great achievement itself.

During meditation, contemplate the various blessings that have been bestowed upon you. As you contemplate, you will realize the immense grace you have already received.

7

THE PRELIMINARY RITUALS

PREPARE YOUR BODY

If we believe that whatever is inside our skin is "I,"
and everything outside our skin is not "I,"
then meditation breaks this belief.

When a child learns to ride a bicycle, he first practices in a tragc-free area that is large, flat, smooth, and safe. The place can be a driveway, a walkway, a school ground, or an empty parking lot. Once he becomes comfortable with riding and is able to maintain balance, he is encouraged to ride in the midst of tragc. Soon he is able to ride in a busy street, the marketplace, or anywhere.

The same happens in meditation. After carefully preparing our body and mind, we initially begin our meditation practice in a suitably peaceful and comfortable environment. While we gain expertise in this practice, we also train our body-mind. We then find that we can meditate anywhere, in any situation, even in the din and roar of the marketplace. Let's understand the preparation required at the body level now.

PREPARE THE BODY

1. Body posture

Whenever the mind is restless, the body responds by becoming hyperactive too. As a result, it is hard to keep the body still. However, if we make the body stable, the restless mind may also settle down. Therefore, for meditation, the posture should be such that the body remains steady. Choose a body posture that is convenient and comfortable so as not to have tension in any part of the body. Some example body postures are given below.

Padmasan

Sukhasan

Vajrasan

Sitting on a chair

If there is tension in any part of the body, then as a consequence there can be tension in the mind too. Someone who is a beginner in meditation should refrain from meditating in a horizontal or standing posture. In horizontal posture, there is the possibility of falling asleep. In the standing posture, we may soon become tired. Therefore, sitting is the best posture for meditation.

2. Position of sitting

In the practice of meditation, the posture of the backbone is of utmost importance. While sitting, we should ensure that we keep our backbone straight, without tension, and at a ninety-degree angle to the ground. The backbone should neither be over-tense in order to keep it straight nor totally relaxed to cause it to bend during meditation. By avoiding both extremes, we should balance the backbone at such a point that the effect of gravitational pull is uniformly spread over the body. The resulting gravitational pull of the earth is minimal on the body in this state, enabling us to sit in meditation for a longer time without getting tired. When the gravitational effect is unevenly distributed across the body, it causes pain.

Keeping the backbone straight while walking, standing, or lying down is also important. If we allow it to become habitually bent or crooked this affects our confidence, induces laziness, and will cause further hindrance in meditation.

3. Mudra (Symbolic hand gesture)

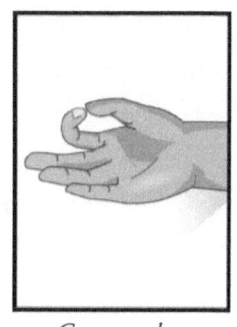

Mudras are hand positions associated with energy flows in the body and can be helpful in meditation. There are many *mudras*, but the Gyan *mudra* or Wisdom posture is considered to be the best. This *mudra* is made by bringing the thumb and index finger of the hand together, while the remaining three fingers are

Gyan mudra

kept straight. We can make the *mudra* as we like, either with one hand or with both hands. After making this *mudra*, we can keep our hands over the knees, or on the lap just like the "Buddha posture."

Every time we meditate using the same *mudra*, the state of meditation and the *mudra* become associated. The mind receives an auto-suggestion and instantly calms. The body also acknowledges this signal for settling into the meditative state. After some practice, just by using the *mudra*, we are immediately transferred into a peaceful, meditative condition. This happens automatically wherever we are and whatever we are doing.

If you have to face an interview, the *mudra* will help to boost your self-confidence, concentration, and memory. If your memory fails you during an exam, the peaceful state created by the *mudra* may help you to remember. During any critical decision making, you may use the *mudra* to help you take the decision from a composed disposition. If you are stressed or anxious, the *mudra* will take you to a relaxed, tension-free, and calm state. If you should receive any shocking news, you may adopt the *mudra* to induce peacefulness.

4. Body movements before meditation

Our brain is actively at work when we are busy performing daily tasks. However, when we sit in meditation the brain needs to lower its frequency. Therefore, as a rule we need to slow down our activities for at least ten minutes before meditation begins. During that time, we should perform every activity patiently, in a slow, calm, and committed manner. For best results, we should plan our daily schedule so that we can avoid any stressful activities before meditation.

5. Body movements during meditation

Maintaining the same body posture without moving, if possible, helps us to get into the depths of meditation and prepare for its highest state. However, if you experience physical discomfort or have been advised by a doctor not to sit in a given posture for long, then you may certainly move the body. It's better to move the body than to abandon meditation. People who are in pursuit of mystical powers tend to torture their body by not moving. Yet this is not meditation.

With continued practice, we gradually learn the art of meditation. We understand what the needs of meditation are through our own experience. Thereafter, the body naturally reduces its own movements. We get settled in the experience of the Source. When we operate from the state of being, body movement will happen spontaneously without need for judgment on whether movements are right or wrong. In this state, we can maintain the same experience even when our eyes are open or we are walking.

6. Body movements after meditation

We should try to minimize body movements for some time after finishing meditation. Slowly get up and walk in a natural way. Let things happen on their own. Don't hurriedly get into any action.

7. Keeping the eyes open or closed

We should practice meditation with eyes closed so as to go deep within meditation. With open eyes, it is possible for the mind to become entangled in external objects. If we intermittently happen to open our eyes in meditation, then we should sit facing a blank wall without pictures or patterns so as to cause minimum distraction.

If we particularly wish to meditate with open eyes, then we should practice by focusing on one spot or on a particular fixed object that is of no interest to the mind. Such meditation increases concentration power and inner strength.

8. Breath

Breath-watching has long been regarded as the best aid to start meditation. Breathing should be normal while meditating. There is a deep co-relation between the breath and the mind. We breathe rapidly when we are angry or our mind is upset. We breathe slowly when the mind is calm. This works equally well the other way round. When we breathe slowly, the mind calms down.

9. Physical purity

Some people may choose to bathe in the morning before meditation. This is an optional choice. However, try to wear comfortable, loose clothing for meditation.

10. Diet

Meditation can be practiced most easily in the morning and evening when the stomach is empty. At other times, a balanced, light diet is always helpful for meditation to prevent any tendency to fall asleep during practice.

11. Duration

As a beginner, it is recommended to sit in meditation for at least 20 minutes. Out of these 20 minutes, a beginner will spend the first 5–7 minutes calming down thoughts. The last 5 minutes or so might be spent thinking "Is it time to get up now?" In between this, there are actually only 5–7 minutes spent on meditation. However, consistent practice will enable this period to increase naturally on its own.

Some people may fear that if they dive deep into a timeless state they may spend an hour instead of 20 minutes in meditation. Those with a busy schedule that could be disrupted are advised to set a buzzer before meditation. They can then meditate in a relaxed manner without worrying about time.

REVERSE WORDS MEDITATION

Sit in the meditation posture with a proper mudra and close your eyes.

1. In this meditation, you should try to pronounce individual names in reverse order. For example, by reversing the name "Tom," you will say "Mot."
2. Try to reverse every name you are familiar with.
3. While doing this, you will need to concentrate your mind completely, otherwise you will find the practice difficult to accomplish.
4. Consistent practice of this meditation will help you improve your concentration. This increased concentration will help you later to reach the depths of contemplation and meditation.

Things you need to be aware of:

1. At first, you may not take this meditation seriously. You may consider it to be simply a fun activity. However, the purpose of this meditation technique is to improve the concentration of your mind. Therefore, it is not to be treated merely as fun.
2. While reversing the names, your mind may sometimes feel content and sometimes discontent. However, without labeling your achievements as "good" or "bad," continue reversing the words.

WALKING MEDITATION

So far, we have learnt meditations that are practiced while seated. Now we will practice a meditation that can be followed when walking. You can practice it easily while walking anywhere. You may find this technique very simple, but it has many benefits. Let's understand this meditation technique now.

1. Breathe normally while you are walking.

2. While you are breathing, repeat in your mind first "IN-2-3-4" (this means you should breathe in till the count of 4), then "OUT-2-3-4" (this means you should breathe out till the count of 4). When you are taking a breath, say "IN", and when you are releasing a breath, say "OUT." (You are not asked to say 1, because "IN" and "OUT," are considered as the count of 1.) Repeat this process in your mind as you walk. To illustrate it more clearly, keep repeating while walking: "IN-2-3-4… OUT-2-3-4… IN-2-3-4… OUT-2-3-4…" In this way, you can practice meditation together with your morning walk.

3. If your breathing is deeper than this, then you can increase the count to 5 or even 6. If your breathing is shallower, then you can count just to 2 or 3. With your mind focused, you will be able to practice this meditation properly.

4. Ensure there is a rhythm between "IN" and "OUT." This means that your breathing and your walking should be naturally in tune.

5. Choose a place for this meditation where you will have no disturbance or hindrance so you can focus only on your counting.

6. If you lose track in your counting then simply begin the count again. Continuous practice is key to the success of this meditation.

When you are walking somewhere, and there is a pole or other object some distance ahead, you can practice this meditation until you reach the object. You should practice this walking meditation according to the rhythm of your breathing, while also paying attention to your footsteps. Notice your breath as it comes in and goes out. Ensure your breathing continues normally and naturally. If you try to adjust your breathing according to your steps, then you will get short of breath. This feeling of shortness of breath is natural when practicing the meditation for the first time. But gradually, with consistent practice, the problem will be resolved. Then it will become natural for you to practice this meditation rhythmically. You will experience the disappearance of all other thoughts during this meditation practice.

You can benefit from this meditation in the following situations:

1. When we are in the midst of people we sometimes have fearful thoughts, such as: "People are looking at me. What is going on? What should I do now?" We become disturbed when such thoughts arise in the mind.

    But if you have developed the art of concentration then your attention won't focus on these thoughts. For example, if you are going to an interview and you feel nervous, you can practice this walking meditation. It will help you to walk confidently into the interview room. Anybody watching you won't know that you are practicing meditation. Instead they may think, "What a personality! What a confidence!" No one will know that you were scared.

2. Some people hesitate to join in parties because they feel uncomfortable in the midst of others. Even if invited to accept

an award on stage they will try to avoid it. At such times, they can practice walking meditation. Thereafter, with this practice, they will feel confident about attending a party or stepping onto a stage.

3. Students can also benefit from this meditation. If thoughts intrude and disturb while you are studying, take a break for two to three minutes and practice this meditation. If it is not possible to walk, you may just close your eyes and focus on your breathing.

In addition to the situations mentioned above, you can practice this meditation at any place or time that you choose. Please read the instructions carefully before practicing. With consistence practice, you will get to know where and when it needs to be used. Once you learn it properly, you can receive its benefit throughout your life.

This meditation is regarded as very important for increasing levels of concentration. You have been given just a glimpse of this meditation. Try to practice it at least once a day and assimilate it into your life.

8
ATTAIN DEEPER ATTUNEMENT
PREPARE YOUR MIND

We speak to God through prayer and
God answers our prayer through meditation.

Waves originate from the ocean, sustain there for some time, and then perish back into the ocean. This cycle goes on incessantly.

Our mind is similar to these waves. Thoughts arise from the ocean of Consciousness. They sustain there for some time and then perish back to the ocean again. No thought is permanent. Infinite thoughts run through our mind from morning to night. We exhaust much energy by giving attention to these thoughts. When we sit in meditation with such a mind, it won't allow us to go deeper within. Hence, it is necessary to prepare the mind before beginning meditation so as to attain deeper attunement. Let's understand how we can prepare our mind to go deeper in meditation.

PREPARE THE MIND

Relax the mind.

It's better to slowdown activities before meditation so that the mind becomes relaxed. Before the time for meditation, tell the mind, "I was in a hurry earlier, but now I am going to slowdown my activities." For the best results, plan your daily schedule in such a way that you avoid any last minute rush.

The mind can be relaxed by observing the breath. You don't need to regulate your breath. Neither do you need to breathe rapidly nor take long, deep breaths. Breathe naturally while meditating. When breathing is slow the mind becomes calmer.

Perform prayer before meditation.

Prayer has tremendous power. It can cool the pyre of worry. It can stop a storm. It can bring a sinking ship ashore. Prayer invokes the happy desire to be liberated from all other desires. When we are free from all desires, we attain a thoughtless state in which true understanding awakens. By performing prayer at the beginning of meditation, we surrender all our problems and worries into the hands of God. We then become receptive to the grace bestowed upon us during meditation. It is said that we speak to God through prayer, and God answers our prayer through meditation.

You can pray in whatever way you are accustomed. You may use your own words. The appropriate feelings associated with prayer can be invoked through certain gestures, such as joining palms near the heart or any other body gestures you are familiar with. Before performing your chosen prayer, you can perform one more prayer to make yourself receptive. It is called the Bright prayer. It is an invocation for the meditation to bear positive fruit. The Bright prayer is as follows:

> The prayer I will now recite will have the most positive effect on my body and mind.

Now, repeat the prayer you have chosen in which you have faith. Alternatively, you may repeat the prayer given below with rhythm, complete peace, love, deep feeling, and full faith. This prayer has tremendous power to relax your mind.

> I am peaceful in the presence of God (Silence).
> I am experiencing complete peace.
> I am created by God.
> Therefore peace and happiness,
> which is the nature of God,
> is spreading within my heart and mind.
> God has created nothing to disrupt this peace.
> Whatever may be the reason of my unrest
> is not in the list of the Almighty.
> I am surrendering myself in his lap just like
> a tired child rests in its mother's lap.
> Waves of happiness are arising all around me and
> I am feeling a sense of peace everywhere.
> Peace ... Peace ... Peace....

3. Contemplation

Contemplation is a technique for focusing the mind. Certain difficult things can be easily understood through contemplation. If we try to think over a topic at length, our thinking will tire after time. Contemplation enables us to think on a topic to the exclusion of all other topics and beyond our normal limits. Without contemplation, we would not realize the value of even the priceless spiritual knowledge that we have gained. It would remain as mere information to us. Without contemplation, even diamonds are mere pieces of coal. Every stone when polished with the tool of contemplation has the possibility of becoming a gemstone.

When we contemplate upon topics which lead us to deeper truths about life and our true nature, our mind becomes conducive to access inner silence. The purer the contemplation, the faster we reach the state of stillness within. However, if we contemplate on other topics that lead us to the external world, then the mind tends to become cluttered, making it difficult to access the inner silence.

As practice, you may contemplate some of the example topics given here.

A. How was your face before you were born?

B. How was your face before your parents were born? (If you keep thinking this over, initially you could get the wrong answer, but later you may get the right answer.)

C. Every person should take some calculated risks. This helps in progressing further.

D. Instead of not taking any decision, it's better to take a wrong decision and learn from it. Those who take wrong decisions gain experience and learn the art of making right decisions. This indicates that their "wrong" decisions were not in fact wrong.

E. Death is a long sleep; and sleep is a short death. Don't die before dying. Instead of dying every day out of fear, it is better to die only once in life.

F. The strength to fight problems has been given to us before the problems arise. Even before a child is born, nature has made arrangements for its milk.

G. Every bad person has some good qualities and is rewarded because of them.

H. One who is free from luck is lucky. God (Consciousness) is present within everyone. Then who is not lucky?

I. Sorrow does not appear in your life to make you unhappy. Sorrow comes to awaken you.

J. Arousal of desire is not the cause of sorrow. When the mind becomes identified with desire, then it becomes the cause of sorrow.

4. Consistency and continuity of meditation.

Meditation should be practiced regularly and consistently. We should meditate at least once or twice a day. There should not be even a day's break, as this can become the cause for laziness. As continuity increases, the mind becomes accustomed to meditation. As soon as we sit in meditation, the mind immediately becomes calm and reaches into meditation's depths. Meditation becomes an integral part of us just like breathing. In the future we will reap the benefits.

5. Instruct your mind before meditation.

Instruct your mind to be patient during meditation, without being concerned whether the state of Samadhi is attained. The mind may imagine about that state and will check whether that state is attained. It may believe that the meditation session is successful only when a thoughtless state is reached. If there are painful sensations on the body or if we fall asleep during meditation, the mind may assume the meditation session to be a failure. However, instruct the mind before meditation that no such thing is true. Successful meditation is that in which thoughts, body sensations, and emotions are observed from the perspective of a detached witness. Self experience is possible, regardless of the presence or absence of body sensations and thoughts. Therefore, there is no need to worry about the results or keep checking for them during meditation.

During meditation, thoughts related to new ideas or solutions to the problems may arise and the mind may start thinking over them. Instruct the mind that separate time can be given for them, although they may be of interest to it. The present time should be utilized only for meditation. By practicing meditation, Self is given opportunity to know itself.

The mind may mechanically perform meditation as a ritual or may get stuck in the technique itself. Therefore, tell the mind not to be stuck in meditation techniques. With proper understanding, the mind becomes ready to surrender during meditation.

NUMBER MEDITATION

It is important to understand the inner workings of the mind in order to be in tune with it. This meditation is helpful in bringing the mind and the intellect in harmony with the Source. It improves concentration so as to enable going deep within. First read the instructions of this meditation and then practice it.

1. Sit in the meditation posture with a mudra and close your eyes.
2. Now visualize a pair of two-digit numbers and multiply them. For example: 47 x 22.
3. While multiplying, do not use any mathematical trick or memory technique. Do it in the same way as you would do the math on paper, but in your mind.
4. When you have the answer, open your eyes. Now solve the problem on a piece of paper to check whether your answers match. In this example, the number 22 was chosen, that is, 2 and 2, which are identical digits.
5. If you have not succeeded with the first experiment, then try a second. By keeping your eyes closed, complete the calculation of 47 x 47. Since 47 and 47 are the same numbers, there is less possibility of forgetting or calculating incorrectly.
6. Now try to mentally calculate the answer to 47 x 29. Try to understand the purpose behind these mathematical calculations. Getting the correct answer is not of the greatest importance. The purpose is to improve alertness and concentration while the mind is performing the calculations.
7. As part of this meditation, if you are unable to multiply two-digit numbers you should begin with single-digit numbers. As

you become confident, you can easily multiply two double-digit numbers.

8. If you are able to multiply two-digit numbers easily you can proceed to multiply two three-digit numbers. When you are able to tackle these easily, then you can move on to higher digit numbers.

Different states experienced during the meditation

1. If you dislike numbers you may experience boredom while practicing this meditation. You may think of abandoning it or of not practicing this meditation at all.

2. If you like numbers you will be able to multiply the numbers quickly and will finish the meditation early.

3. It's possible you might actually find it easier to multiply the numbers in your mind than on paper.

You will experience one of these states during the meditation. If you feel troubled during the practice, always remember its purpose. The purpose is not just to multiply the numbers, but to learn the art of increasing concentration through this technique. Be very clear about the purpose so that you can complete the meditation regardless of any hurdles.

Benefits of meditation

1. How did you find this exercise of improving concentration? Were you able to focus on the numbers for some time but then your concentration slipped away? With this type of mental exercise, you can strengthen your concentration and mental power, which is useful for reaching into the depths of meditation.

2. Did you have any thoughts during the exercise? You might have observed that other thoughts disappeared during the exercise. This is exactly its importance. You have learnt the art

of being in the present while practicing this meditation. When other thoughts arise, they are related either to the past or the future.

3. With this meditation, you will learn the art of being in the present as well as the art of relaxing the mind. The mind becomes exhausted with its continuous running around and incessant thinking throughout the day. If you learn the art of meditation in the right way, then you will learn the secret of how to remain fresh at all times.

9

ROADBLOCKS IN THE JOURNEY
THE HURDLES TO CROSS

Meditation is for annihilating the ego.
Not for perpetuating the disease of ego.

Consider a mall in your neighborhood that provides a spectacular panoramic view from its rooftop terrace. Imagine it is the talk of the town, with people sharing their experiences of deep and everlasting peace and bliss when they witness the view from the terrace.

As a teacher on summer holiday, one fine morning you decide to experience this vista yourself. However, as you enter the mall, a troupe of familiar children flocks around you. They plead with you to tell them a story and won't let you go until you do. As you finish one story, they insist you tell another and another. Eventually you manage to escape and hurriedly board the escalator to go upstairs.

Tired and now hungry, as you reach the first floor another group of school children gathers around you. They oger to share their food. Being famished, you readily tuck in and stop only when you are satiated. Now your energy has returned and you thank them. But as you start to move on, they insist you to listen to their poems. You cannot deny them. They start singing their poems aloud. First one, then another, then another.... Your energy slowly begins to wane. Somehow, you manage to escape. But now you are in a dilemma over whether to progress or abandon your journey. You are only six floors from the panoramic view so you decide to move ahead. You climb the staircase hoping you will now find some solitude.

On the next floor, you see an empty, peaceful corner. You sit there in meditative posture to calm yourself. But before a few minutes pass you hear a loud whisper in your ear, "Sir, please. Please look at our paintings." Now, you are fed up! You open your eyes and see another group of small children around you. Oh no... not again! The thought of viewing their paintings frustrates you so much that you rush to the ground floor and exit the mall.

We go through similar experiences when we commence the journey of meditation. On such a journey, it is inevitable that we encounter roadblocks on the way. At first, we may feel impatient to make speedy progress. This impatience is a form of craving or expectation. If we don't notice changes happening or progress seems slow, we can begin to develop an aversion for the practice. Finding our predefined expectations are not being met, we may get depressed, or vexed, or begin to make excuses to avoid meditating. If we start feeling that meditation is a waste of time, then we may doze off soon after starting practice, we may doubt our own capabilities, or we may lose confidence in the meditation technique itself. When faced with such roadblocks, we may even think of abandoning the journey!

At such times, we must understand that every meditator has to go through these difficulties. With perseverance, these impediments gradually disappear. When we attain the right understanding and adopt the right attitude, we can deal with these roadblocks and make progress.

We can then reach the ultimate goal of meditation – the terrace of the mall of life! We too can then experience the state of love, bliss, and peace that has been sung about and praised by the enlightened ones. Let's understand the roadblocks we face in detail now.

ROADBLOCKS IN THE JOURNEY

1. Disappointment

Some people approach meditation with a goal-driven attitude. After consistently practicing meditation for a few days, they expect to see tangible benefits in their life. They want to experience such objectives as peace of mind, tranquility, deeper intuition, or greater creativity. If they don't immediately see such results they become disappointed. They begin to believe that meditation is not helping them, that it is a futile exercise and a waste of their time. At this point, many may quit the practice.

The key is not to hold any expectations of meditation. The art of meditation is just to be present, and allow any and every feeling or thought arising to pass by.

2. Self-Doubt

In the initial stages of the journey, we can experience self-doubt and many questions arise. We ask: "Am I meditating correctly? Can I meditate as easily as others do? Can I meditate for long enough? Will I be able to share positive experiences? Am I really suitable to practice meditation?"

When we become impatient about wanting changes to happen, we start doubting our capabilities. But such excessive self-analysis merely creates stress and distracts us from the main goal of meditation. Some may move from one school of meditation to another in a vain attempt to overcome their doubts. What they don't realize is that as long as doubts continue in the mind, changing meditation school serves no purpose.

3. Restlessness

Sometimes we find our mind is racing during meditation. Thoughts about the recent past or the near future constantly occur in our mind. Such thoughts may even consume our entire meditation session. Many people assume that meditation itself is to be blamed for this, thus consider it to be unhelpful and abandon the practice. We should understand that this problem is a reflection of the restless mind and not a consequence of meditation. Engaging in intense activity before meditation leaves our energy levels high. When sitting in the stillness of meditation, our mind stays attached to such energetic thoughts. It is only through meditation that we become aware of this restlessness of mind, which would otherwise go unnoticed.

4. Boredom

The mind plays no role in meditation. We just need to sit and do nothing. As a result, we may struggle with a feeling of boredom. At first, a few minutes of meditation might feel like we've been sitting for an hour. If we are unable to accept this, meditation may seem difficult to practice, and we might even consider quitting.

It's important not to give up at such moments. Continuing to practice despite uncomfortable feelings brings its reward. We shouldn't resist feelings of boredom but rather accept them as part of the practice. We should continue to meditate and watch such feelings as a detached witness. As we persist with meditation practice, such feelings of boredom pass away.

5. Lethargy

Sometimes, as a beginner, we feel too lazy to sit for meditation. We may consider it a waste of time and turn to other activities. Even if we sit in meditation, lethargy can overpower us and we start to doze off. The mind reasons, "As I'm not able to meditate properly, I'll leave it and just go to sleep." Succumbing to this mental logic we abandon the practice.

We should understand that the mind deceives us with logical excuses all the time. As soon as we become aware of this habit and reject it, it no longer troubles us. Thereafter, when the mind complains that nothing is happening in meditation, tell it, "Even if nothing at all happens, I will meditate as planned." If the mind still tries to get its way, then get up, splash cold water on your face, and resume meditation. Resolve to meditate for the decided period every day, regardless of obstacles or excuses. Make this your goal.

6. Ignorance

The real purpose of meditation is to experience who we truly are. The real "I" is beyond the body, mind, and intellect. It is the Source of everything. It is beyond form, shape, size, and boundaries. It is the boundless expanse of pure awareness. However, in ignorance we believe ourselves to be a limited, individual personality. Unconsciously, we get entangled in this personality's tendencies and habits. We harbor defilements like anger, boredom, comparison, depression, ego, fear, greed, and hatred. Instead of being happy in the present, we seek happiness in the past or future. We lead a constricted life.

Meditation helps to break these limitations. Consistent practice of meditation builds our conviction that we are separate from the body-mind mechanism. It helps us appreciate that we have received the body-mind mechanism in order to open ourselves up, blossom, and play the divine play that God is enacting on earth. By being who we truly are, we become the Source of joy.

7. Sense Objects

As soon as we court the pleasures of the senses we lose ourselves in them. Our ears are absorbed by melodious music. Our eyes are captivated by enchanting sights. Our tongue craves delicious tastes. We are intoxicated by sweet fragrances. We get lost in the feeling of delicate touch. Our mind revels in intellectual delights. In short, we seek out and constantly entangle ourselves in all kinds of sensual pleasures. However, all these are roadblocks in our journey of meditation.

We are deluded into believing these sense objects are merely for our pleasure. But for those seeking enlightenment, they are a means to direct our attention to the knower. In spiritual terms, this process can be called "Self-Witnessing." Such external sense objects are the means to Self-Witnessing and thus stabilize us in our sense of being or the Self.

Viewing the world informs us that we have eyes. Hearing sounds informs us that we have ears. Experiencing tastes, smells, and touch should also remind us of the true purpose of our five senses. Rather than our attention being absorbed by the objects of our senses, they should lead us to awareness of the presence of the senses themselves.

As our senses stimulate thoughts in the mind, we should be aware of the knower who is witnessing those thoughts. The knower is always awake, aware, and conscious of those thoughts. Our sensory perceptions are signals to connect to this supreme Source of knowing. It is due to ignorance that we accept the illusion of our perceptions but miss the news of conscious presence that they are constantly conveying to us. As a result, we are fixated on knowing all that our senses perceive instead of knowing the knower of everything.

These hindrances are nothing but the teething troubles that occur only in the initial stages of meditation. If we consistently meditate despite such hindrances, this phase will soon pass away. We then attain subtler depths of meditation and can easily meditate for a longer period. As we derive the bliss that is inherent in meditation, we become convinced we should practice daily, just as we are convinced we should wash every day. With the passage of time, whenever we get the chance, we take the opportunity to dip into inner stillness. Nobody will even notice as we briefly connect within, but the effect makes our life unfold easily and effortlessly.

"ATTENTION ON ATTENTION" MEDITATION

"This is a clock, this is a wall, this is a window, this is a curtain…" This is the way we generally look at things around us. However, as part of this meditation, you won't be looking at things the way you usually do. This meditation will transform the way you look at objects.

1. Look at all the objects around you. After thoroughly looking at the first object, examine the second object, then the third object, and so on.

2. While observing these objects, closely notice where your attention gets stuck, where it quickly slips away, where it gets defused, and where it gets disturbed. Understanding all these aspects of your attention is called "attention on attention."

3. Having practiced the above with open eyes, now close your eyes and feel the environment around you. Is it cold or hot? Are you experiencing stiffness in your legs? Is your body tired? Are you feeling sleepy? Feel everything.

4. Now know through direct experience that although you are with your body, you are not your body. Being "with your body" implies that the body is your companion. Now observe every sensation arising in your body and tell yourself, "This sensation is happening in my body, not with me."

5. Keeping your eyes closed as you continue to practice this meditation, observe where your attention gets stuck, and where it slips away.

You will feel refreshed after practicing this meditation. What is your attention? What makes it change? What does it move away from? What does it chase? What makes it stuck? What does it let go? You will have answers to all these questions after this practice.

The important thing is that you learn to be attentive about your attention.

Practicing this meditation gives proper direction to your thoughts. Those thoughts that incessantly run in your mind will automatically cease. This practice will improve your awareness, and you will gain subtle knowledge about your attention.

10

DISTRACTIONS IN THE JOURNEY

BEWARE OF ALLUREMENTS

Wealth is a path, not the destination.
Meditation is the destination, not a path.
Wealth is everything, yet nothing.
Meditation is nothing, yet everything.

There was once a king, whose subjects would often say, "Oh King! We rarely see your great majesty. Kindly bless us with your presence." Eventually, the king agreed and said, "Very well. I will meet you this Sunday at the assembly ground." Accordingly, the king organized a fete with free entertainment and stalls ogering all kinds of free food for everyone. All his subjects gathered at the ground on Sunday. The king arrived too and sat expectantly in his tent. As all the entertainment was free, many people became preoccupied with playing games, eating food, and making merry. Only a few went to meet the king. Before, people had complained that they could never meet their ruler. But, how many really wanted to meet him? How many were truly keen for a sight of the king?

Many embark on the journey of meditation. But, how many truly attain the ultimate goal of meditation? Many get stuck in the distractions that arise on the way. When we are convinced of the ultimate goal, we will neither be content with temporary relief nor entrapped by such enticements. Let us now look at the distractions in this journey.

DISTRACTIONS IN THE JOURNEY

1. Mystical powers

During meditation, the latent powers of the body are awakened. As a result, the mind becomes focused and concentrated. A focused mind, by itself, is a tremendously powerful force, which can generate great achievements. However, some people may divert this power to awaken Kundalini energy, or for astral travel. Thus, instead of progressing further in the path of meditation, they become distracted by such mystical powers.

2. Healing practices

Meditation is helpful and effective in treating disease. Diseases such as asthma, high or low blood pressure, paralysis, and many others, have been noted to improve with the practice of meditation. Meditation has definite positive effects on the mental and physical planes; however, simply achieving better health is not the goal of meditation.

If we stop the practice of meditation at the experience of a relaxed state of mind, its solace and its joy, we deprive ourselves of attaining the true goal of meditation. Hence be alert. You may get lured by the superficial benefits of meditation and make them your final goal. These intermediate benefits may influence you so deeply that they become all you seek.

3. Meditation rituals

The sense of presence is so subtle, and so close to our essence, that it can be difficult to experience. Furthermore, we don't experience it immediately upon closing our eyes for meditation. Hence, from ancient times, various rituals of meditation have been devised to encourage the experience. Many people practice rituals such as breath-watching, or concentrating on the third eye (the point between the eyes), or watching changes occurring in the body to attain experience of the Self. However, as we get into deeper meditation and experientially come to know the Self, such rituals are no longer required. Unfortunately, some people get rooted in such rituals in the name of meditation and don't progress further.

4. Boosting of the ego

While practicing meditation, we may get engrossed in arousing latent powers so as to feel superior. As a result, the ego gets boosted and we become arrogant and egoistic. There cannot be a bigger mistake than this. It leads us to stray from the basic goal of surrendering our ego and thus knowing who we truly are. Such enticements impress us with knowledge but result in depriving us of realizing the ultimate truth for which we are actually striving.

NEUTRAL MEDITATION

In Neutral Meditation, you remain neutral about every thought. If you feel sorrow, you remain neutral; if you feel joy, you still remain neutral. Let's first understand the method of this meditation.

1. You can practice this meditation with eyes open or with eyes closed.

2. First, sit in a meditation posture, and let your breathing be natural.

3. As initial preparation, ask yourself, "Why are you seated in meditation? What will you be doing during meditation? What could possibly happen during meditation?"

4. When you have considered these initial questions and are clear about the answers, then you can derive full benefit from the meditation session.

5. If you feel sad during meditation, don't say, "I am sad." Instead, tell yourself, "Thoughts of sadness are passing through my mind." If you are happy, you should remain neutral. Simply tell yourself, "Thoughts of happiness are passing through my mind." In this way, you should watch every thought that arises in a neutral manner, and tell yourself simply that such a thought is passing through your mind. Just as news headlines or advertisements scroll past in the strip at the bottom of your TV, treat thoughts also as scrolling past your attention. Watch these thoughts as you would watch the scrolling news on your TV screen.

6. Remain neutral, whether your thoughts are of happiness or sadness. Since you are asked to remain neutral regardless of any states in this meditation, it is called "Neutral Meditation."

You can practice this meditation at any time of day, regardless of your condition. When thoughts of boredom or laziness arise in your mind, practice this meditation. Just tell yourself that thoughts of boredom or laziness are passing through your mind. When thoughts of hatred arise, watch them also with a neutral feeling. Tell yourself simply, "Thoughts of hatred are passing through my mind." This meditation will help you remain balanced and detached in every situation.

11

OBSTACLES DURING MEDITATION

PITFALLS IN THE PRACTICE

Meditate on the one who is meditating.

*A*carnival procession is trouping through the main street of town. To get a better view of the procession, you visit your friend, whose balcony looks onto the street. Many people are gathered there with you to watch the colorful procession.

As you watch, some children behind pull your shirt and poke you with noisy questions. You can't concentrate on the procession. Unwillingly, you answer them. But, they don't stop there. They have more and more questions with which to disturb you. In agitation, you leave the balcony and go to the neighbor's apartment to view the procession. There, some elderly people, constantly coughing, also ask you questions, but they can't hear your answers. Youngsters in the house have put on loud music and you have to shout to make yourself heard. Soon, you feel distracted by all this noise and decide to move on to the next apartment.

Here, you find you have the unlikely pleasure of listening to these householders' angry quarrels. You can't enjoy the procession from their balcony either. So, as a last resort, you visit the last apartment with a balcony over the street. The ladies there are troubled by their noisy children and are busy scolding them loudly. So, now what can you do? Every household you visit disturbs you one way or another.

In this story, the building represents our body-mind. When we sit in meditation, we use the body-mind as a medium to experience the Source. This is signified by the witnessing of the carnival procession. However, after a while we become distracted by the thoughts of the restless mind. This is represented first by children who keep distracting attention. They conjure thoughts of fear and ambition, which pull us out of the meditative state. Next, we experience discomfort in the body, which is symbolized by the elderly people. Aches in the legs, shoulders, or spine distract us from the peace and bliss of meditation. Fighting neighbors represent feelings of hatred and ill-will. Indulging in thoughts over arguments and making comparisons with others prevent us from experiencing the Source. The ladies who scold their children represent thoughts of attachment. Thoughts of attachment towards objects or people cloud the clarity of our mind.

Finally, the street represents life in this world. When we lack proper understanding, worldly obstacles distract us from the experience of the Self. However, with right understanding, the same obstacles become instrumental and serve as a medium to know our original state of being.

As we lead our life, we go through a variety of experiences. These trigger a whole range of emotions such as anger, anxiety, attachment, boredom, confusion, depression, doubt, ego, fear, greed, guilt, hatred, ill-will, impatience, insecurity, jealousy, and lust in our body. We either express these emotions or we suppress them.

When we sit in meditation, the conscious mind, which has been active all the time, slows down. We become aware of subtler aspects of the body-mind mechanism such as the breath, emotions, thoughts and various body sensations. We also witness a train of thoughts and emotions passing through us. Certain thoughts trigger our suppressed emotions within. They manifest as pleasurable, painful, or neutral sensations on the body. During meditation, we should witness these thoughts, emotions, and sensations with equanimity. We can then be liberated from them forever. When we react to these emotions, by favoring them or resisting them, they are reinforced rather than being released. Indulging in these emotions then gives rise to further thoughts. Thus, the cycle continues.

When a thought of anxiety arises, we add further thoughts to the worry. We remember pending activities and start feeling concern for them. When we become aware that we've been distracted we focus again on meditation. Then some new ideas arise, which we feel we should remember but fear we will forget. We may begin to reflect on incidents that give rise to feelings of ill-will or hatred. We may be distracted by thoughts of fear, greed, jealousy, or insecurity. We may feel overcome by feelings of boredom or lethargy. We may become distracted by recurrent self-checking to analyze our state, or become absorbed in taking credit for achieving a thoughtless state.

These recurring thoughts may then give rise to doubts

that we are meditating correctly. We may start to compare the ongoing meditation session with a previous meditation we've had. If we find too many thoughts are racing through the mind, we feel dissatisfied not to be experiencing an earlier peaceful state. Thoughts of depression then add themselves to our mental worries. We may begin to feel we are unworthy or incapable of reaching a higher spiritual state. Random thoughts of these kinds continue to arise in the restless mind. As this happens, we forget that we are seated to witness these emotions, thoughts and sensations and use them as a medium to access the Source within.

As part of our preparation, we should consider the way to handle all these obstacles before meditation. Then during meditation, we should witness them with equanimity, alertness and understanding. Regardless of the variety of emotions, sensations of pleasure or pain on the body, or thoughts of craving or aversion, we should have the underlying understanding that these are temporary. They have emerged, will remain for a while and will then subside. Therefore, instead of indulging in them, we should use them as an instrument to know the knower of everything. This way, we can break free from them and abide in the sense of being.

As we progress in meditation, new dimensions begin to unfold before us. Some people report that in meditation they have seen a blue light, heard a cosmic sound, lost sense of the body, or such experiences. They try to anticipate and fix such results in their next session of meditation. However, every session of meditation is different. If we try to fix the end result, then we will be disappointed. It is important to understand that these are merely milestones in the journey and we need to progress further without getting stuck in them.

A TO Z MEDITATION

Now, we will practice A to Z meditation to understand the tendencies of the body-mind mechanism.

Our body-mind is intended to be used to experience the Self and to express our divine qualities. Is this what the body-mind is actually doing? Or is it becoming a hindrance due to laziness, lethargy, lust, disquiet, impulsive behavior, or some other limitation? In the following table, using the alphabet from A to Z, examine what actually affects your body-mind. This honest enquiry of your mind will bring to light all its tendencies. These habits not only drive your behavior while you are awake, but they also dominate even during meditation. When you become aware of them, it becomes easier to get rid of them.

A	Ambitious	The mind is Ambitious.
B	Blind faith, Beliefs	The mind is full of Blind faith, Beliefs and Superstitions. It gets entangled in these and is not interested in understanding the truth. By understanding the truth, blind faith is gradually transformed into unshaken faith.
C	Credit taker	The mind is Credit taker. It greedily takes credit for the work it has accomplished and loses the opportunity to know and serve the truth. It thinks, "Let me take the credit first, I will think about the truth later."
D	Delusion, Deceitful	The mind gets entangled in Delusion. The sensory perceptions of the illusory world entrap the mind and deviate it from the truth. The mind is Deceitful. It deceives others and even deceives itself.
E	Egoistic	The mind is Egoistic.

F	Fifty-Fifty mode	The mind works in Fifty-Fifty mode. It has a divided loyalty between truth and illusion. Its focus is divided between virtues and vices. It can't become one-sided.
G	Greedy	The mind is Greedy.
H	Hasty	The mind is Hasty and impulsive. It does not like to wait. By working hastily, it loses awareness.
I	Impersonator, Intellectualist	The mind acts like an Impersonator. It assumes various masks and plays multiple personalities. It gets entangled in various forms and shapes. The mind is an Intellectualist. Its habit is to apply logic and to reject anything illogical.
J	Jealousy	The mind is full of Jealousy, ill-will and envy. It envies others and wants that which others have acquired.
K	I-Know-It flaunter	The mind acts like an "I-Know-It flaunter." It likes to show off its knowledge, and it listens to truth believing that its understanding is better than others.
L	Lazy	The mind is Lazy. It obstructs progress. Its delays lead us to lose opportunities and fail to achieve accomplishments in life.
M	Mechanical	The mind functions Mechanically. It gives predetermined responses according to its past conditioning. Considering the mind to be no more than a machine prevents us from enjoying the pleasant journey of attainment of truth, which is pleasant at the beginning, middle, and end. People who serve like a machine can't enjoy this journey. Those who are attentive overcome this.

N	Non-believer	The mind is a Non-believer. If prayers are not answered, the mind becomes disappointed with God; it experiences disbelief and may become Atheist.
O	Opposite viewpoint	The mind has an Opposite viewpoint. It views everything through the spectacles of the illusory world. It sees everything through the filters of its preconceived notions and beliefs and adopts negative viewpoints.
P	Political	The mind is Political. Just as politicians create troubles for themselves and others with their selfish motives, the mind tries to balance truth and the illusory world, and seeks benefits from both.
Q	Questioning	The mind is a Questioning mind. It gives more importance to asking questions than knowing the answers to those questions.
R	Regretful	The mind engages in Regret over incidents that happened in the past. It feels disappointment when repeatedly remembering past mistakes.
S	Slow learner	The mind is a Slow learner. There is no problem in learning slowly, but it risks maintaining consistency. The mind needs resolve to increase speed to reach the goal.
T	Teacher	The mind is a Teacher. It is more interested in teaching than learning.
U	Untrustworthy	The mind is Untrustworthy and deceitful. It cheats itself as well as others.

V	Vigilant	The mind is Vigilant and aware. It does not get entangled in the illusory world. It is awakened through the practice of meditation. This awakening contains laughter and joy, faith and generosity.
W	Workaholic	The mind is a Workaholic. It can't remain quiet. It is hyperactive. It always wants to think. Such a mind cannot sit still, or rest, or sleep.
X	eXtremes, X-ray	The mind likes to dwell in eXtremes. Either it wants to eat in excess or eat nothing, to talk endlessly or not talk at all. By choosing extremes it avoids the stable, middle path. The doubting mind likes to conduct an X-ray of everything by analyzing unnecessary details and finding fault.
Y	Yearning	The mind Yearns for sensual pleasures and gets deluded in lust. Just like pigs like to roll in mud, the mind likes to dwell on, and wallow in, lust and fantasy.
Z	Zero	The mind begins with a Zero (nothing). Practicing meditation consistently, contemplation, and listening to discourses and reading literature on truth, will all help attain the formless Zero.

SECTION III
ADVANCING FURTHER

12

STAGES IN THE JOURNEY

TRANSFORM YOUR MIND

Consistency is the hallmark of success.

*Y*ou have been looking forward for many days to meeting your dearest friend. Finally, the day has arrived. You take time out from your busy schedule to meet him at a market square. Six of his friends also accompany him. As you reach the market square, you first see these friends and you start chatting with them. You get so engaged in conversation that you forget you were there to meet your friend. Your friend respects your wishes and calmly observes you, but doesn't interfere. Soon time is up and you have to leave. Then you regret not giving attention to your friend because you unnecessarily spent your time with the others.

This is exactly what happens when a beginner starts the practice of meditation. We sit in meditation with the goal of experiencing the Source within. However, as our mind is untrained we spend most of the time thinking about past or future events. We think about our problems and possible solutions. Or we linger over memories of sensual pleasures. When the time comes to end our meditation session we regret spending this valuable time in such futile pursuits. This may lead us to think meditation is a waste of time and consider abandoning the practice.

We need to understand that although the purpose of meditation is to access the Source within, our mind may not be trained enough yet to immediately support us in this endeavor. Along with consistent meditation practice, training our mind can support us in this journey of meditation. Let's understand the various stages involved in training the mind so that we can complete the journey and attain our goal.

1. Clearing the mind

Clearing the mind is of the first importance. The mind is always entangled in thoughts. Either it dwells in the past, or it wanders in the future. It never likes to stay in the present. In the first stage, we have to bring it from its multitude of negative thoughts towards positive thoughts. To the extent possible, hatred and ill-will have to be removed from the mind. Forgiveness and tolerance should be practiced. The mind should be purified by listening to the Truth. The mind should keep thoughts of well-being for others.

> Where negative thoughts end,
> "Happy Thoughts" begin.
> Where there are Happy Thoughts,
> the mind becomes pure.
> Only a pure mind can drop into
> a thoughtless state.
> Being in a thoughtless state leads to
> the experience of Self-realization.

Without purity of mind, if any capacities or powers are achieved, then the mind becomes egoistic instead of being subdued.

Hence, the mind should be purified when you begin this journey. As meditation evolves towards Self-Meditation it will be easier to keep the mind pure, but efforts are required in the beginning to instill the mind with qualities like kindness and compassion.

You can practice following forgiveness prayer every night before going to bed.

> I forgive everyone with
> a big heart and complete purity.
> I forgive all those who have hurt me
> knowingly or unknowingly today.
> By doing this, I am not doing a favor to anyone, but myself.
> I am raising my purity of mind
> and elevating my consciousness.
> I am bringing happiness and
> prosperity into my own life.
> With God as the witness,
> I sincerely seek forgiveness from all those whom
> I may have hurt through my feelings,
> thoughts, words or actions.
> Please forgive me; I will try my best
> not to repeat this in the future.
> I will take care of this.
> Thank you for forgiving me.
> Dear God of Justice, please help me to forgive myself.
> Please help me to accept myself.
> Please help me to love myself.

Purity of mind is given importance in every sect, creed, and religion of the world. For example, the rules for control over the body and mind such as Yam-Niyam, the five cardinal principles of life called as Panchsheel, brotherhood, worship, prayer and so forth, have been devised for keeping the mind pure and peaceful.

2. Watching the Mind

With a pure mind, we now need to understand how to watch the mind in order to learn its behavior. We can't see a breeze, but through the movement of leaves, we can know of its presence. Similarly, if we want to know the mind, then we should look at its thoughts. Thoughts convey the most useful information. In this stage, every thought has to be watched, but without becoming identified with or lured by any thought. This is the most important stage in transforming the mind. Be aware that it is also where we can succumb to many errors and misunderstandings. Watching thoughts requires persistence if they are to be properly understood. Let us try to explain this with an example.

> *When we first watch a movie we notice only the most obvious aspects. Our attention is focused on our favorite actors and the plot. When we see the same film for a second time the experience is different. We notice many more details. Now our attention may change towards the characters in the background or the locations chosen to shoot the film.*

It is the same with the mind. If we watch the mind again and again, we can gradually uncover its secrets. Each time we observe it we can notice new things and achieve greater understanding. For those who begin to understand the mind, life becomes easy. There will be peace, tranquility, and harmony in life.

3. Taming the Mind

In this stage we control our mind, not with force but with patience and understanding. If we force the mind to become quiet during meditation, it rebels and thoughts increase. The mind habitually holds onto old ideas and indulges in imaginings. It can demand to see divine light, to witness the blissful image of Lord Shiva, or experience the cosmic form of God. We must keep all such imaginings, expectations, and assumptions aside, and meditate without anticipation or judgment.

Thus, before beginning meditation we should ignore past experiences. Tell the mind, "I do not know or expect anything. Let me see what I experience this time." We can then meditate peacefully in a relaxed manner.

Understanding our thoughts helps us to master them. We just need to remember that we are meditating. While meditating, if we get caught up in thoughts about work to be completed for example, then the mind is our master. This could lead us to a feeling of aversion towards our thoughts and make us treat them as an enemy. However, rather than regarding thoughts as an enemy, we should consider them as our ally. Thoughts actually help us. They remind us that we are not concentrating and that our mind has wandered elsewhere. During meditation, we only need to be aware. Thus, we should use thoughts as a reminder to be aware of and know our true nature.

During meditation the most important thing to experience is that there is someone present. Even in the absence of thoughts, who reports that we are thoughtless? A thought emerges to inform us, "I have been thoughtless." Without this thought, we would never know that our thoughts had ceased. At this stage, we learn to make thoughts an instrument to help us experience the presence behind our thoughts. Now the mind starts behaving as a good servant to who we truly are, and it becomes still and tranquil.

THOUGHT NUMBERING MEDITATION

1. In this meditation, thoughts are eliminated by giving sequential numbers to them in order to reach a thoughtless state. Begin the meditation by watching every thought.

2. Now start numbering each thought. As soon as one thought arises, number it in your mind as "one." Wait for the next thought to arise. As the second thought arises, number it as "two." In this way, continue counting thoughts.

3. Watch, as your thoughts come and go and let them continue in a normal, natural manner. Some thoughts may be positive, some negative, some related to work, while others may be thoughts of boredom. Whatever be the thought, count them regardless of the type of thought that arises.

4. You may get thoughts regarding this meditation itself, "What is the use of this meditation?" or "This does not seem to help." Just give a number to each of such thoughts as well and then await the next thought.

5. Continue to sit quietly even when there are no thoughts. If the thought arises, "At this moment, I don't have any thoughts," then number this thought too because it is also a thought.

6. Do not pursue any thought. Just number each thought and leave it. Your mind might wander away and pursue a trail of thoughts instead of numbering. If this happens, whenever you remember, start from '1' all over again.

7. The number of thoughts that arise can reduce significantly with this meditation. A thoughtless state can result. Practice this meditation regularly without expecting a given result.

13

EXTERNAL TRAINING

TRAINING ON GROSS ASPECTS

*Effort is required to become something that
we are not, to attain what we do not have.
Being what we already are is effortless.*

*A*n *elephant-tamer rides his untamed elephant through the busy
streets of the marketplace. The elephant, being untamed, puts its
trunk into many stalls selling fruits and vegetables. The elephant tamer is
unable to prevent the elephant from troubling the hawkers and ravaging
their stalls. However, after the elephant-tamer has trained the elephant,
he returns to the same marketplace, and together they now smoothly pass
down the street without causing harm to the hawkers and their stalls.*

Our body-mind is like the untamed elephant. Because of its inherent tendencies and habits, it causes harm to others and in turn also to us. When we sit in meditation, thoughts, feelings, and body sensations distract us. When we train our body-mind, it behaves like the obedient elephant. It then serves as a medium to access and experience the Source within. We can then abide in peace, bliss, and love in and through all life situations. Let's understand the training required at the body-mind level now.

TRAINING AT THE BODY-MIND LEVEL

1. Train your focus.

We should focus on what we want, not on what we don't want. When we focus on the vices of others, we tend to absorb those vices. As a result, our mind gets contaminated. Such an impure mind doesn't allow us to go deeper in meditation because it drains our energy. When we focus on people's virtues, our mind is cleansed. With a tranquil mind we can go deeper in meditation. Every person is a combination of vices and virtues. But we should focus only on the virtues. This training in turn helps us when we practice meditation. When emotions and feelings, thoughts and body sensations distract our attention during the practice, we should choose to focus instead on the Source.

2. Train the senses.

In our usual lives, our senses are entangled in the sensual objects of the external world. Our eyes are fixated with the captivating sights of people and things. Our ears yearn for melodious music, entertaining gossip, pointed criticisms and news of the world around us. Our tongue craves relishing all manner of appetizing tastes – and participation in discussions that give us intellectual pleasure. Our skin pines for a soothing and comfortable touch. Our nose seeks out sweet aromas. With all these attractions, we become completely engrossed in the external world.

But now we need to train the senses. Ask yourself, "Where is my attention?" If the attention is fixed on aspects of the illusory world, say "Turn within. Now where is my attention?" This will help train our senses to turn inward to our joyful, subtler nature.

With this, our level of awareness will rise. The senses can then serve as a medium for the Source to experience itself. Any sound the ears hear will remind the Source of itself. Any sights the eyes see are a reminder of the divinity within, which enables us to witness those sights. Any touch the skin senses is a reminder of the sense of presence that exists beyond thoughts. Any taste the tongue savors is a reminder of the enlivening principle. Any word the tongue speaks serves as a reminder of the ultimate truth of our existence.

3. Get rid of SICK programming and develop the power of discrimination.

We have become victims of SICK programming since our childhood. In this case, SICK is an acronym for Sorrow borne out of Ignorance acquired during Childhood due to Krazy beliefs. It is inherited from our parenting, our neighborhood, our media and our surrounding environment. It is Krazy (with a "K") to indicate that the inherited beliefs we hold are baseless and the result of incorrect interpretation of incidents since childhood. This is also called past conditioning.

Our parents and neighbors play an important role in this. They may not have been trained to focus their attention properly. As a child, we saw them glued to the television watching serials or movies. We saw them engrossed in gossip and criticism about food, clothing, entertainment, and people. We saw them enslaved by the latest fashion trends. We saw them ecstatic on receiving sensual pleasures and distressed when they were denied. At that tender age, we didn't have our own power of discrimination. Hence, we just learned and copied what we saw. Not for a moment did we doubt that the programming we'd received could be wrong. We believed it to be our own natural thinking. We never considered the source or the basis of our choices in life. Thus, our happiness solely depended upon external circumstances.

But now we should witness this SICK programming within us. We must identify our past conditioning and get rid of it. We should make decisions based on the wisdom we have received, and the power of discrimination that has awakened within us. With this, we can permanently remain in the state of love, bliss, and peace, regardless of external pressures.

4. Maintain consistency in meditation without anticipating end results.

Consistency is the hallmark of success. This also holds true for meditation. Those who have consistently practiced meditation have attained the ultimate truth. They have relentlessly practiced a fixed period of meditation every day, over many years, without seeking any results. Others would have given up the practice, but they persisted and achieved the ultimate benefits. This is best exemplified by famous inventor Thomas Edison.

Edison was an American inventor and businessman. He was responsible for over 1,000 digerent patents, some refinements of previous inventions but many completely new ideas. Edison is famous not only for his inventions but also for his attitude on failure. In his mind failure was simply another stepping stone on the road to success.

For Thomas Edison each failure was just one step closer to fulfilling a goal. He also said, "Every wrong attempt discarded is another step forward." He was credited with many patents for the inventions made as part of his failed attempts.

Unlike the average person, Edison continued to try and try again. The famous story goes. Edison failed to refine the light bulb 9,999 times. Just imagine if he had given up after the 9,999th time! A journalist asked him, "How does it feel to have failed 9,999 times?" Edison replied, "I haven't failed. I have had great success finding 9,999 ways not to invent the light bulb."

If we allow setbacks to paralyze us, we begin to lose hope, we become cynical, and our lives suffer. We, alone, can decide for ourselves what path we are willing to take, the path of a winner or that of a loser. Like Edison, we also need to stick to our goal. For that, we need to consistently practice meditation.

As a beginner, we should be cautious that our mind doesn't constantly interrupt to check whether we are benefiting from the practice. Instead of trying to discover whether we are experiencing a sense of being, we should simply be consistent in the practice. When we practice meditation in the right way, we are bound to receive the desired result.

5. Train your body movements.

Some people have the misconception that they need to remain in meditation for many hours without moving their body. They believe that in the advanced stages of meditation, they may need to stand for a prolonged period, with swelling feet, but not move their position. Or that they may be required to sleep only in a standing position. Such beliefs may prevent many people from venturing into meditation.

We should understand that following such rigorous techniques is a different path – and not the path of Truth. Keeping the body steady is just a means to train ourselves for the highest state of meditation. A steady body helps us to calm the mind, and it is the calm mind that helps us go deeper in meditation.

A beginner may experience physical discomfort by sitting in one position for a fixed period. At such times, it is better to move the body rather than abandon the practice itself. With consistent practice, we can gradually learn the art of relaxed meditation. A time will come when we understand what meditation requires through our experience. Then, concerns over not moving the body will be gone. The body will reduce its movements automatically when it operates from the state of presence beyond thoughts. We will not need to consider if body movement is right or wrong because it will not affect our state. We will even be able to remain in the same state with eyes open or when moving.

Those who suffer from physical ailments should always abide by their doctor's advice and not strain their body for too long. They should feel the freedom to move their body whenever they feel physical discomfort.

6. The first 10–15 minutes of meditation is merely the preparatory period.

Many people ask whether it is suitable to reduce the duration of meditation after consistent practice. The answer is that when we begin the practice of meditation we are asked to meditate for a longer period because the mind doesn't quiet immediately. Most of our time is spent dealing with thoughts about the external world and physical discomforts. Only after sitting for some time do we actually get into the depth of meditation.

Thus, in the initial stages, we should consider the first 10 to 15 minutes as preparation for meditation. Only after the preparatory period of calming the mind can meditation begin. Gradually, with practice, this preparatory period reduces. Later on, we may reach the depths of meditation as soon as we sit for practice. However, even at such times, it is advised to continue practice for a full period of time so as to be prepared for the next stage of meditation.

The next stage of meditation, the timeless state of Samadhi, begins after the preparatory stage. We need to remain in a state of meditation for some time to observe what is happening. Know what is happening by remaining in the state of being.

THOUGHT WATCHING MEDITATION

When people sit in meditation, they are often overcome by a deluge of thoughts. People are unable to break out of the habit of compulsive thinking. This leads to a constant feeling of discontentment and incompleteness within. They are unable to detach from thoughts and feelings.

The key purpose of this meditation is to de-focus from the content of thoughts by letting them pass by and saying "Next." This way, you allow thoughts to pass by so that they do not hold your attention

1. Close your eyes and sit in the meditation posture.
2. Watch your thoughts as they pass by. Don't judge them. Simply observe them. Let them continue in a normal, natural manner.
3. Continue watching them from a distance like a witness (i.e., without getting identified but remaining detached). By separating yourself from your thoughts, you will know what kind of thoughts go on in your mind.
4. Some thoughts may be positive, some negative, some may be related to your work, while others are created out of sheer boredom. Keep your body steady and focused regardless of the type of thoughts that arise.
5. Do not label thoughts as good or bad. Avoid desires such as, "I want more thoughts" or "I don't want any thoughts."
6. Watch every thought, let it pass without chasing it, and silently utter the word "Next." The word "Next" acts as an anchor, allowing thoughts to reach their natural conclusion and dissolve.

7. Saying "Next" also raises your awareness of the gap between the thought that's receding and the next thought that's appearing.

8. This interval may be as minute as a thousandth of a second, but focus on that point regardless of the length of time. In that interval there is no thought... everything has stopped and is frozen in that moment. In this gap, you continue to know the silence by being a detached witness to it.

9. You don't need to be worried if you miss the gap; instead, simply pay attention to the next thought and allow it to pass.

10. When you meditate but don't see any immediate results, you may become disappointed. The mind, in turn, may respond through an inability to concentrate. Focusing on thoughts of disappointment, though, will only drain your energy.

11. The key is to just watch these thoughts as if they were dark clouds passing by – clouds that are far away that don't affect you. Observe these thoughts with a detached feeling, as if you are a "witness" watching them from afar.

12. As you continue watching thoughts with "Next", number of thoughts may reduce. However, don't consider the meditation session to be a failure if the number of thoughts doesn't reduce. In fact, successful meditation session is that in which you witness thoughts in the right way so as to get the glimpse of the Self-witness. Self is already thoughtless. Thoughts are used as a medium to know it.

13. When thoughts of disappointment occur, never say, "I am disappointed." You are not your emotions; you are experiencing them. Instead, say, "Thoughts of disappointment are passing through my awareness." Simply dismiss them by saying "Next" and move on to watch the next one.

14. Similarly, when you feel boredom, never say, "I am bored."

Instead, say, "Thoughts of boredom are passing through my awareness." Allow them to pass by saying "Next".

15. Initially practice this meditation for five minutes then gradually increase this time.

THOUGHT INTERVAL MEDITATION

You may practice this meditation separately or along with thought watching meditation. In this meditation, you should focus on the interval between thoughts. Let's understand the method of this meditation.

1. Close your eyes.
2. Focus your attention for a while on each part of your body.
3. Now start watching your thoughts. Concentrate your attention on them. See your thoughts coming and going. Let the thoughts continue in a normal and natural manner. Some thoughts may be positive and some negative. Some thoughts may be related to work while others may be of boredom. In every state, keep your body steady.
4. There is an interval or gap between the thought that is receding and the next thought that is arising. This interval may be a thousandth part of a second, yet concentrate your mind on that interval or that point. (In this interval there is no thought, everything has stopped or frozen in this moment, everything is silent.) Decide in your mind that you will continue knowing the silence between two thoughts with the feeling of a witness.
5. If you miss the gap, do not worry; pay attention to the next gap. Keep inspecting yourself. Through the gap between two compartments of a train passing through a station, we can catch a glimpse of the opposite platform. In the same way, we can catch a glimpse of the Self-witness through the gap between two thoughts.

You will feel fresh after doing this meditation because the energy that is spent on thoughts is conserved.

14

ART OF WITNESSING

KNOW THY SELF

Understanding is the seed;
Meditation is the fruit.
Truth is the seed;
Remembrance of God is the fruit.

There is a village. When people enter this village, arrows are shot randomly at them from any direction. While they walk along, somebody may aim an arrow at them… somebody may throw a stone at them… or somebody may throw dust in their eyes and run away.

If anyone visits the village for important reasons, he must face an interview at the village entrance. The interviewer gathers whether the visitor is capable of staying in the village safely or will get hurt. He knows that if the visitor enters without any training, he will be injured and will return wounded. Therefore, he assesses the visitor's ability to quickly spot arrows shot at him and so escape. Thus, the interviewer plays an important role.

If a visitor is considered insugciently trained to enter the village, the interviewer trains him to develop his attentiveness. He makes him aware of the particular sound made by an arrow when it is shot. By developing his attentiveness, the visitor is able to catch that sound and escape the arrows that are randomly fired at him. With this training, he can visit the village safely and return unhurt. Let's understand the deeper meaning of this analogy. The village symbolizes the illusory world. Arrows indicate the onslaught of testing situations in life. When we are not alert while going through these situations, we suffer. We are hit by the arrows of the illusory world.

When someone abuses us and we retaliate, it means we have been wounded by an arrow of illusion. When we later realize our mistake, we feel regret and think, "I should not have reacted this way. I should have been attentive." Such grieving over a sorrowful thought means we have been wounded by the arrow of sorrow. When we are driven by our tendencies, it is like being attacked by arrows.

This analogy also depicts what happens when we are seated in meditation. During meditation, various thoughts, emotions and body sensations arise. They are like arrows shot at us. But if we are not trained to expect and handle them, we believe them to be real and react to them according to our past conditioning. As we react to them, we become distracted from meditation. Becoming injured by the arrows symbolizes a drop in the level of our consciousness.

When we undergo the internal training of meditation, we learn to deal with these arrows in a proper way and we return unhurt. The training not only helps in meditation, but also helps us to safely pass through the many testing situations of life. We become more attentive and sensitive towards the arrows shot at us, and we can deal with them creatively instead of becoming their victim. We can thus remain happy amidst all life's situations. Let's understand the internal training in detail now.

THE ART OF WITNESSING

During meditation, dormant past impressions, ingrained within us from behavior learned since childhood, become activated and appear in conscious awareness as thoughts, emotions and body sensations. We tend to either suppress them or express them according to our past conditioning. However, as part of internal training, we should just observe them with the art of witnessing. With the art of witnessing, we neither express our triggered programmed reactions nor suppress them. We just witness them as they truly are. With true witnessing, they are permanently released from our body-mind. As a result, our body-mind gets truly purified. Here, witnessing doesn't mean seeing with open eyes. Witnessing is just knowing our reactions and being aware of them.

True witnessing involves the following three essential aspects.

1. Understanding

The core understanding is that "the one who we truly are" is separate from the body-mind. We are the Source who is using the body-mind as a medium to know itself and express its divine qualities. During meditation, our body-mind becomes cleansed and begins to serve as a mirror for the Source to know itself. Understanding implies a firm conviction that all the thoughts, emotions and body sensations that arise are happening with the body-mind… not with us, the one who we truly are.

The other key aspect of understanding is to know that everything that arises at the level of the body-mind is temporary. It is fleeting.

> *Every thought or feeling is like a flare shot into the night sky. A flare is a trail of light that rises up in the night sky, exists for a few moments and then dissolves into the dark.*

In the same way, thoughts and feelings arise from the presence that we truly are. They show up for a few moments, or a few minutes, then dissolve into the silent stillness in the background. We need to develop a firm conviction about the temporary nature of all thoughts and feelings. Then we will not give undue importance to them or react indiscriminately.

2. Awareness

If we are unaware during meditation, we may lose ourselves in thoughts, emotions and body sensations. The mind spends most of its time in fantasies and illusions. It chews over the experiences of the past. It attempts to re-live either the joy of the pleasurable experiences or the worries and regrets of the unpleasant ones. As a result, we become distracted from meditation. If we develop the ability to be aware of the present moment, we can immediately detach ourselves from these distractions and focus on the Source.

> *Just like a cat that waits with all its attention focused on a mousehole, ready to pounce when the mouse appears, so we should be aware of the changes in our body-mind. Witness those changes and immediately focus on the Source.*

3. Equanimity

This is the ability to witness all the thoughts, emotions, and body sensations for what they truly are. Treat everything with an attitude of evenness; an alike manner which is beyond like and dislike, aversion or craving. We should look at pain and pleasure, praise and blame, success and failure, fame and shame with evenness. We should understand that they are temporary. They have come to go. While they are there, just watch them with equanimity.

THE SENSE OF THE BODY AND THE SENSE OF BEING

Two songs are being played simultaneously. We are asked to listen to only one song and not confuse the two together. Initially, we find it digcult, because sometimes our attention goes to one song and sometimes to the other. However, when we concentrate our mind on just one song, then we can successfully listen to that song alone.

In meditation, we become aware of the sense of our being through the medium of the body. The sense of the body and the sense of being co-exist. There may be painful sensations on the body. Despite these, we need to focus our attention on the sense of being.

It is incorrect to equate the success of meditation with the loss of body sensation. If the sense of the body is lost during meditation that is a bonus, but it is not an actual aim. However, people can become entangled in this aim through misunderstanding. Had it been true, people suffering from pains would have never attained Self-realization. In fact, we can focus on the sense of our being despite painful sensations on the body.

Every night we lose the sense of the body when we sleep, yet we are not delighted with it when we get up in the morning. Merely losing the sense of the body is of no use if there is no understanding. People have many such experiences, but inwardly they remain the same. Therefore, during meditation we should pay attention to the sense of being, and not to the sense of body (or lack of it). Before meditation, we should instruct ourselves not to be disturbed by the sense of body remaining during meditation. We can then meditate with ease.

> *Consider the body as like a fan that is beside us blowing air. If the fan is removed, we can't feel the air. Likewise, if the sense of the body is removed, we will not be able to experience the sense of being.*

The body is helping us to sense our presence every moment. We are the sense of pure being; the body is only a pretext to know our true nature. In ignorance, we assume the limited form of the body to be our nature. However, our true nature is boundless, vast, much beyond the limited confines of the body. As the body is helping us to know our nature, give it a pat on the back and say, "You're doing a good job. Keep sitting next to me so I can experience who I truly am and express my qualities through you."

Nevertheless, if there are habits, tendencies and disorders in the body, the body will not support us during meditation. It will react according to its old programming, and we will find ourselves lost in the details of the body-mind. We will get entangled in thoughts, emotions and body sensations and become distant from the sense of being. We need to work on the disorders of the body – to break its tendencies and habits – in order to stabilize in the experience of the Self.

We need to prepare our body as we would inculcate good behavior in a child. With repeated teaching of understanding and rewards for behaving well – thereby we can learn. A day will then come when we will affirm, "Whatever state arises in the body will be merely an entertainment; I will enjoy it."

When we are seated in meditation, we become aware of the breath, thoughts, emotions and body sensations. Let's understand how to deal with them in the chapters that follow so as to make the body instrumental for the experience of the Source.

BREATHING MEDITATION

Breathing indicates that the body is alive. In order to lead life in a better way, there are various techniques frequently recommended with regard to inhalation and exhalation of breath. Very often, such techniques are unnecessarily linked with spirituality and Self-realization. While practicing these techniques you need to understand that breath is related to the body, and by working on breath you can improve health. However, true spirituality is not related to the controlling of breath; it is different from that. Practice the following breathing meditation to improve your concentration.

1. Sit in an appropriate meditation posture.

2. Relax yourself by taking one or two deep breaths and releasing them slowly.

3. Subsequently, let your breathing continue to be as it is at present. Shallow breathing or deep breathing, comfortable, natural – however it is, let it continue. If you try to control your breathing then it is not meditation. It is Pranayam (breath regulation).

4. Be aware of whether the breath is going in or coming out. Now it goes in… now it comes out… from the right nostril… from the left nostril… or from both nostrils. Be aware of every direction and every state (cold or warm) of the breath.

5. Practice this meditation for 20–45 minutes as convenient. After some time, when you become an expert in this meditation, you may meditate on the interval between two breaths using Breath Interval Meditation.

DIFFERENT STATES EXPERIENCED DURING THIS MEDITATION

1. While practicing the above meditation, your focus may suddenly shift from your breath to your thoughts. This can often happen at the beginning of the meditation. If this occurs, then bring your attention back to your breath. By returning the focus, continue with the breathing meditation. Consistent practice will make you proficient.

2. Similarly, while practicing you may find your attention pursues sounds that you hear, like the tune of a song or the sound of a bird. However, remember that you are not supposed to chase after any sound. You just need to focus on your breath.

3. With this meditation, you will get to know many truths about your breathing. For example, if your breath is short you may try to stretch it. But, don't do this. You are only required to pay attention to your breath in this meditation. If you wish to control and direct breath to improve your health then you may choose to practice Pranayam. However, as part of this breathing meditation, just pay attention to your breath and don't try to guide it.

BREATH INTERVAL MEDITATION

You may practice this meditation separately or together with the breathing meditation. In this meditation, you should focus on the interval between your breaths. In today's busy life, no one has time to wait. However, if you can simply become aware of the interval between breaths, it can deliver remarkable growth in stamina. Recognition of the interval between breaths will later help in realizing the experience of the Self (Feel in the blank). Therefore, don't treat this meditation as any ordinary meditation. Rather, treat it as a pathway to Self-realization. Honestly practice it every day. Let's understand the method of this meditation.

1. Begin this meditation in the same way that you began the breathing meditation. Be aware of the breath moving in and out through the nostrils.

2. After observing the breath for some time, try to be aware of the interval when the breath is neither going in nor coming out. Now, concentrate your mind on that interval (point). Feel in the blank, don't fill in the blank!

3. When the breath moves in, it stops for some time. Try to focus on that interval or gap. Make a firm resolution in your mind that you will be fully aware of the interval where the breath changes its direction.

4. Let your normal breathing continue during this meditation. Don't try to regulate your breathing. If you miss any of these intervals, there is no need to worry. Pay attention to the next interval between breaths.

5. Our breathing continues all the time. Therefore, there is no time limit for this meditation. You can practice this meditation anytime, anywhere.

You may find this meditation very easy to practice. Or, at first, you may feel like regulating your breath. However, remember that you are not intended to control your breath in the breath meditation technique. If you regulate your breath, this will be *Pranayam*, not breath interval meditation. Simply continue to breathe naturally.

15

WITNESS YOUR THOUGHTS

INTERNAL TRAINING – 1

You cannot do anything to become thoughtless because you have always been thoughtless since the beginning.

WITNESS YOUR THOUGHTS

During meditation, we can find that thoughts of the recent past or the near future are incessantly running through our mind. New ideas may also arise. Pursuing these thoughts distracts us from meditation. It's only when we regain awareness that we realize we have been distracted. If we don't attain a thoughtless state, we may consider our meditation session a failure.

TRAINING TO WITNESS THOUGHTS

1. *We should understand that the body is a thinking machine. Thoughts keep running through it. There is no knowing what thoughts may arise. A new thought can pop up at any moment, and we get entangled in it. We feel these thoughts in the same way as we feel the presence of clothes on our body. We feel them on our*

body just as we feel the air from a blowing fan.

These thoughts are very much a part of the body. However, the one who we truly are is separate from the body. We need to practice to see how the body becomes an instrument to know the Source.

2. We should watch thoughts arising in the body from a detached point of view.

    If a note with the word "Anger" was stuck on your forehead, how would you perceive it? You wouldn't feel the emotion. You would only feel the presence of the note. Whatever word was written on the note, it would not agect you. You would only sense the note. This sensing would itself be a reminder of your sense of being.

    Similarly, we need to look at our thoughts in the way we would feel the note. Watch all the thoughts and emotions arising within the body and tell yourself, "Whatever thoughts and emotions make their presence felt, they only remind me of my sense of being."

3. *We should witness thoughts in the same way that we watch files opening in a laptop. When we open a file in our laptop, it does not mean it is opened within us. That file is simply opened in the machine we are using.*

    In the same way, thoughts and emotions are like different types of files that are being opened in the body we are using. They occur in the body, but we are separate from the body. We are the Source. Once we are established in the conviction of this truth, through direct experience not just with the intellect, we will be able to quickly detach ourselves from emotions and thoughts.

4. *We should witness thoughts in the same way as we witness children playing from a distance. When two children fight with each other and the third one complains about them and defends himself as a*

good boy, we should treat this child as a part of the same bunch of children without giving undue importance to this child. Tell the child, "You too are one of them."

While meditating, thoughts of anger or hatred may arise. At that time, another thought will inform us about these thoughts. Then we should consider that thought as a part of the scene. With this, we will be able to remain in the state of pure awareness. Even while we are in this state, suddenly a thought may arise, "What a beautiful state this is! I have never experienced such a peaceful state before." Understand that this thought too is trying to distract us from the state of pure awareness. Again, treat it as one of those many thoughts.

5. In order to defocus from thoughts, we should focus on our breath. As we focus on breathing in and breathing out we become aware of the present moment.

The mind plays tricks that can divert us from our journey. The checker and the credit-taker are the biggest obstacles. Let's understand how to deal with these and other such thoughts such as *the questioner* and *the fixer*.

THE QUESTIONER

During meditation, questioning thoughts may occur, such as "Why do I have so many thoughts? When will a thoughtless state emerge? Why do I feel heaviness in the beginning and lightness later on?" Some of these thoughts are simply checking whether we are meditating or have gone to sleep.

Training to witness the questioner

When the mind continuously questions during meditation, this is because the mind has not yet matured in the practice. It is still like a child.

Imagine you are travelling by train with a child who peers through the window and starts asking many questions. "What is this?... What is that?... Why is it this, or that?" You gently answer the questions and enjoy doing so. You don't become engrossed in what the child is pointing out.

In the same way, if questioning thoughts arise, understand that this is normal. Consider it as the mind's mischief, and smile. Treat such questioning as any other thoughts. Without becoming stuck in such thoughts, focus your attention on the sense of being.

THE FIXER

As we progress in meditation, new dimensions unfold before us each day. Sometimes we may feel we have had a particularly pleasant or unusual experience. We then mistakenly want to hold on to this experience, and we expect to be able to experience the same in our meditation again. In doing so, we jump to conclusions and try to predetermine the output of our meditation session. We try to fix the end result.

Training to witness the fixer

We should understand that whatever happens during meditation is quite normal. We should not become fixated about any one thing. Every meditation session is unique in itself. Let whatever is happening happen, and let whatever is not happening not happen. When we are able to know the knower of the result, then that is true progress. If we see a particular light during meditation, then know the seer who is watching the light. If we hear a special sound, then know the knower of that sound. The ultimate goal of meditation is not to know any experiences we may have, but to know the knower of those experiences.

THE CHECKER

When we go deep into meditation, the mind can adopt the form of a checker and try to judge the experience. The checker mind assesses, "Let me see who is experiencing this experience. Is this experience the same as the actual experience of the Self?... Nothing is happening. Therefore, Self is not there... After sitting for so long, why am I not becoming thoughtless?" The mind tries to divert our focus from the experience of the Self by checking, comparing, and judging. If we get entangled in this, we lose our attention on the Source and instead become entrapped by the checker mind. This checking during meditation is the biggest obstacle in our meditation practice.

Training to witness the checker

Whenever the checker mind intervenes, understand that it is a trap. Let's understand it with an example.

> *Someone is inside a washroom. We want to know whether the washroom is vacant. So, we enquire, "Is there anyone inside?" The person replies, "No." Do we then believe that no one is inside or we conclude that there is someone inside? The reply itself indicates someone's presence inside the washroom.*

During meditation, the checker mind questions about the existence of Self. However, the checker mind can't exist without the Source as it originates from the Source. Thus, its very presence indicates the presence of Self. Hence, whenever a checker thought arises, simply smile and observe it. Know that the mind is playing a trick. Understand that we don't have to question our experience; we only need to be present in that experience.

The checker mind tries to distract us by attempting to conceptualize or define our experience.

> *If we have imagined that a doctor should be male, then even after meeting a female doctor, we feel as if we haven't met the doctor.*

Similarly, even after being in the experience of the Self, the checker mind denies the experience of the Self because of its preconceived notions of the experience.

The checker mind tries to assess the experience. It questions, "After sitting for so long, why am I not becoming thoughtless?" It tries to divert our attention towards the painful sensations on the body or thoughts arising in the body. It prompts that the sense of body is not yet lost. It then declares that we are not progressing in meditation. Listening to the checker mind, we may abandon the meditation practice. We need to have a deep understanding of this process so that we can surrender the checker's role.

The checker mind needs to be countered with the understanding that it is enough to witness the play of thoughts, emotions and body sensations in a detached manner rather than determining specific results.

With this understanding we can realize that the checker mind is not qualified to check the experience. The experience of the Self is beyond the domain of the checker mind. The mind can never fathom it. If we believe the checker mind, we will get entangled in it and lose our attention on the Source. Whenever the checker mind appears, instead of fighting it or debating with it, we only need to smile and acknowledge its presence. Let's understand this with an example.

> *You are wearing a pair of spectacles and can see everything clearly. Then suddenly the spectacles start questioning, "Let me see who is watching through me. What is my watcher's shape and form?" You know very well that the spectacles can never see the one that is seeing through them.*

When the checker mind gets triggered, we may need to ask the checker some questions. "Do you know what the experience of Self is like? If not, would you be capable of understanding if explained to you? Is your claim to knowledge within your realm of experience? Or is it only when you are not there that the experience reveals itself?" If we ask these questions repeatedly, the checker will disappear, allowing the experience itself to be revealed. A time comes when the checker becomes mature. It then says, "Now, I will keep quiet. I understand that the experience is beyond my realm of knowing."

Power of faith and devotion help us in and through the process of attaining the experience of Self. Though we have not attained that experience, we should trust abiding by this faith. We particularly need to have faith in the knowledge we have been given about the nature of the checker. Some people find it easy to transcend the checker. Others may need to convince the checker repeatedly. Then the time comes when the checker surrenders out of devotion. It then says, "Thy will is my will." The body-mind then merely serves as a mirror for the Self to know itself and express its qualities.

Until we experience this for ourselves, we need to know that the checker is indeed the biggest obstacle to revelation of the experience of the Self. As we continue with meditation, without asking any questions, we can achieve this conviction in practice. Then we no longer become absorbed by the commentary of the mind. When that happens we move to the next level of meditation. But until then, we need to continue with our practice.

THE CREDIT-TAKER

As soon as we attain the first experience of beingness in meditation, the mind inevitably arrives in the form of credit-taker. It tries to play with the experience and take ownership. The mind says that it owns the experience and will use it for its own benefit. The credit-taker is another big obstacle in our journey of meditation.

Training to witness the credit-taker

Whenever the credit-taker thought arises, understand this is just one more trick of the mind. Make the mind understand, "You can't make use of the experience. It is only when you were absent that the experience was revealed. Therefore, you need to surrender yourself for the experience to be revealed again. To the extent that you remain still, the experience will shine forth. The more you chatter, the greater the delay in attaining the experience of the Self."

When both the credit-taker and the checker surrender, the individual ego ceases to exist. The body-mind then becomes instrumental for the experience and expression of the Source.

We should understand that the journey we have undertaken should be pleasant. Happiness is not just derived from reaching the destination. Hence, it is important to know who is meditating – who we actually are. The one who we truly are is the biggest cause of happiness. So, we need to be happy even while we journey on this path.

"HOW IS MY MIND?" MEDITATION

Read through the instructions first. Then close your eyes and sit in a comfortable meditation posture.

1. Intermittently ask yourself, "How is my mind?" and watch the thoughts arising within you.

2. Witness whether your thoughts are rigid, stubborn, or flexible. Your thoughts may have become rigid due to past conditioning. You might not have re-considered them for many years.

3. See whether the mind is forgiving, giving, grateful, or kind-hearted. Does it feel envious of others' virtues? When does it feel bad or low?

4. When does the mind become your enemy and when does it remain your friend?

5. What does the mind do to get credit? What does it do if it doesn't get credit?

6. Why does the mind not want to relinquish credit?

7. In what situations does the mind imitate others?

8. In what situations does it take a pause for guidance from the Source within?

9. When is the mind unconscious? When is it aware?

10. How many of your thoughts are based on past conditioning? What is the basis for the existence of these thoughts?

11. How can you be free from past conditioning? What habits do you need to inculcate to free yourself?

12. What is the present state of your mind? What are your repeated thoughts? Why are they repeated so often? What will be the thoughts you hold in the future?

13. Why are you sometimes happy? Why are you sometimes sad?
14. When does the ego feel hurt? When does hatred arise? What is the conditioned thought behind such hatred?
15. Slowly open your eyes.

16
WITNESS YOUR EMOTIONS
INTERNAL TRAINING – 2

*Whatever we resist persists, therefore
always focus on what we want,
not on what we don't want.*

WITNESS YOUR EMOTIONS

During meditation, the mind tends to ruminate over thoughts of past and future. Consequently, corresponding emotions get triggered. We may experience anger, boredom, comparison, depression, ego, fear, greed, guilt, hatred, ill-will, jealousy, or lust arising within us. We react to these emotions according to our past conditioning. But this leads us to become distracted from meditation.

TRAINING TO WITNESS EMOTIONS

Whenever emotions arise, we should witness our body sensations and the breath. Our breathing rate and heart rate both increase when we are emotionally aroused. If an emotion of anger has arisen, our breath becomes rapid and shallow. Our ears become warm. The heart beats more rapidly. We feel a pressure in our forehead or in the chest. We feel sudden tension in our arms, neck, or shoulders. These sensations are nothing but the subconscious mind's reactions to the thought that triggered anger. Typically, we tend to identify with these sensations, and because of discomfort and resistance we either burst out into expressions of anger or suppress our feelings forcefully.

As part of our training, as soon as we sense an emotion has arisen within us, we should tell ourselves, "Let me see if this emotion is really being experienced by me or if it has arisen in the body I am using." Through our own experience we can receive the answer that the emotion is happening within the body; not with me – not with the one I truly am. When we are able to clearly see this, then we are in the highest state of meditation.

The body sensations and breathing vary with each emotion. We should witness these changes relentlessly in a detached manner, then see them die down just as waves disappear into the sea. These sensations and our breathing are part of the body; the one who we truly are is separate from them. They are helping us to know the Source.

WITNESS YOUR BODY SENSATIONS

When we sit in meditation we experience various sensations on the body such as heat, cold, heaviness, lightness, dryness, pressure, pain, itching, throbbing, sweating, tickling, twitching, contraction, expansion, vibration, or anything else. We may experience lightness or heaviness on some parts of the body. We may experience painful sensations in our legs, neck, shoulders, or arms. Some body sensations are due to natural body aches and pains; other body sensations arise as an after-effect of emotions. Our past conditioning makes us try to escape these sensations. We may try to change our body posture, scratch an itch, or stretch some muscles. But when we do, we are distracted from meditation.

Training to witness body sensations

We should understand that it is normal for the body to experience various sensations. There is nothing special about them. There is no problem if heaviness in the body persists till the end of a meditation session. Who we truly are is separate from heaviness or lightness.

The sensations we experience are temporary. They have arisen, will remain for some time, and then will perish. Just witness them with equanimity. When we are able to witness these sensations with equanimity it indicates meditation progress. If we like one sensation and dislike another, then it means we have not yet progressed.

In truth, painful sensations we experience are not as intense as we believe. Remove the belief, then experience the pain as it actually is. By this means, we don't need to experience the suffering that comes with painful sensations. Persevere through the pain while the sensation lasts. Pain indicates the release of certain habits and tendencies borne out of past conditioning.

If we resist these sensations, they persist. Therefore, reacting excessively to dismiss transient sensations is a waste of time.

Successful meditation means witnessing all body sensations with equanimity, and knowing the knower of such experiences. The knower is separate from the sensations of the body.

The body is an instrument to know the Source. Defocus from the body to avoid getting entangled in body sensations. Use such sensations as a bridge to experience the Self.

The body is like a mirror for the Self. The condition we find in this mirror helps us to know ourselves. Regardless of mood, memories, weather, or surroundings, the body can become the medium for the Self to experience itself.

Keeping our eyes closed, we have used thoughts, emotions, body sensations, and breath as the means to experience our presence during meditation. Now we will understand how we can remain in this sense of being, irrespective of whether our eyes are open or closed, or whether we are in the marketplace or in solitude.

BODY WATCHING MEDITATION

As part of body watching meditation, notice every smallest thing happening in the body. Notice the sensations and feelings arising in the body. Let's understand how to practice this meditation in detail.

1. Choose a comfortable posture for sitting in this meditation. Maintain a strong intention that you will not move the body during the entire duration of the practice.

2. Watch all the sensations on your body for at least 15 minutes. It is not necessary to watch them in a particular order. You may experience heaviness in some parts of your body. In some parts you may feel an irritating sensation. In some parts you may have a painful feeling. Just watch them as a spectator.

3. After sitting for 10 minutes, you may feel a strong urge to move your legs, straighten or loosen your back, or scratch your face. Resist all these urges and just watch. As you watch, these temptations will go away.

4. If the mind wanders, bring it back and continue to watch the body. You can watch all the sensations successively from head to toe. Or you can simply watch each sensation randomly as it arrives.

5. Body watching meditation requires immense concentration. If you also practice breath watching, then body watching meditation becomes easier to practice.

Things you need to be aware of:

1. In the initial few minutes of the meditation you may experience considerable pain in parts of your body. For example, you may feel an unbearable backache, which could stop you continuing the meditation. If this is a known problem, choose an appropriate seat and posture, and then continue the

meditation. Remember that once you begin the meditation you should only watch the sensations; you should not take any action to prevent them.

2. During meditation, if you experience a pain you have never experienced before, and it happens more than once, you should consult your doctor. In this case, don't consider the pain will eventually subside with meditation practice.

3. While you are watching the sensations of your body, your mind may wander into the past or future. If the mind wanders, immediately return it to the present, and begin watching the sensations again from a witness point of view.

4. After practicing this meditation for many days you may become bored or feel lazy. Always remember that laziness is the enemy of meditation. Don't let it take hold.

This meditation is very effective for gaining control of your body and for improving your concentration. You will come to know its unseen benefits after practicing it for many days. Therefore, try to practice it every day.

17

THE ULTIMATE GOAL

THE STATE OF SAMADHI

*Only God exists; ascertain and
confirm whether you exist or not.*

So far we have learned and experientially understood the difference between the sense of body and the sense of being. We have also looked at the training required to deal with various thoughts, emotions, feelings and body sensations that arise in the body during meditation. Irrespective of these changes, the body can still serve as an instrument to experience our presence.

In fact, we can abide forever in the experience of being, regardless of whether our eyes are open or closed, be it in the marketplace or in solitude, whether we are moving or stationary. Such a state, which is called Sahaj Samadhi, can be attained with the consistent practice of meditation. Indeed, attainment of this state is the ultimate goal of meditation.

Let's now understand Samadhi and its various forms.

We have become familiar with waking, dreaming and deep sleep states. Samadhi is the fourth state, which can be attained through the practice of meditation. Samadhi is the experiential knowing of that which existed before the world was created. Time came later. Time came only after the world came into existence.

FORMS OF SAMADHI

Samadhi in deep sleep state

Everyone, without exception, experiences the state of Samadhi while in deep sleep. But we are unconscious at that time. We are not aware of the hours that pass. We are only aware that we have slept when we wake up in the morning.

During deep sleep we lose the sense of body and experience the state of Samadhi. But after getting up in the morning we again slip into unconsciousness and assume ourselves to be the body. Due to our association with the senses of the body, a world gets created – the world of vision through the eyes, sound through the ears, smell through the nose, taste through the tongue, and touch through the skin. The experience of this world is so intense that we believe earnestly in what is visible and is felt through our senses. As a result, we become completely engrossed in this world and forget the experience of Samadhi we had during deep sleep.

Savikalpa Samadhi

The state of Samadhi available during deep sleep can be made available even while we are aware and conscious by reaching into the depths of meditation. We begin meditation using the practice of Savikalpa Samadhi. Here, we don't experience the timeless state, but we still achieve the state of Samadhi with the help of supportive means. These supportive techniques could be breath-watching, chanting of a mantra, and so on.

As the mind is impatient, it tries to get quick results. It wants to reach the state of Samadhi as soon as we close our eyes. But we need to understand the similarity of this process with the way we drift into sleep.

> We don't fall asleep immediately after closing our eyes. We just need to show our readiness for sleep. There is nothing more we can do to enter sleep.

Similarly, the state of Samadhi can't be fetched. We just need to be receptive and present during meditation. We don't have to do anything. Any supportive measures are intended simply to quiet the mind.

However, we can get trapped in meditation techniques. We may find ourselves continuously checking whether we are progressing towards the state of Samadhi, or whether we have lost the sense of body. But this checking is an obstacle. We need to set aside all such concerns during meditation. We should not expect any result. We should just surrender and be present. We should tell ourselves, "I am receptive to the grace being showered upon me." This way we will progress into the depth of meditation.

The state of Samadhi is mistaken by some as equivalent to sitting with eyes closed for hours on end. Some will sit in yoga positions with eyes closed and feel that they have practiced meditation. They are unaware of the true practice of meditation. Due to ignorance, their mind may only grow stronger instead of being eliminated. It will claim "I went into Samadhi." Thus, instead of being surrendered, the mind also takes credit for something it has not achieved.

In Savikalpa Samadhi we become a witness. We begin by watching and discerning the many things that are around us in the outside world. We become aware of the sounds falling on our ears, the touch felt by our skin, the smells experienced by our nose, the tastes savored by our tongue. Without getting caught up in these sensations, we continue with our practice. Slowly, the witness delves deeper into meditation. We watch the thoughts that are running in our mind, but still we persist with our practice.

Gradually, the number of thoughts reduces. Thoughts involving our imagination and beliefs are dispelled. Checker and credit-taker thoughts are dissolved. By watching and understanding thoughts, the wisdom awakens that such thoughts are serving as a reminder of the witness. The witness then turns into Self-witness. It remembers its true nature of being. At this stage, the state of Nirvikalpa Samadhi is attained.

Nirvikalpa Samadhi

When we use a boat to help us cross a river, upon reaching the other side we abandon the boat. The boat is no longer required for our onward journey.

Similarly, in the state of Nirvikalpa Samadhi there is no need for further supportive means. All such means are no longer required and are released. Only experience, state of being, state of Samadhi, Consciousness, and Self-in-rest remains.

In this state, we experientially know who we truly are. When we arrive in this state consciously, we can attain absolute conviction of our true nature. We realize that we are beyond time, beyond body, and beyond mind and intellect. It is then that the death of the individual "I" occurs and the bright, Universal "I" awakens. The Universal "I" is the Creator within us; the Creator of the world. Spirituality is about experientially understanding the nature of the Creator's existence.

Even after realizing the state of Samadhi and experiencing the eternal bliss within, we find that when we get back into the thick of worldly activities, the mind still looks for security in the external world.

But we need to understand that true security lies within. We need to become stabilized in the experience of Samadhi even when we are engaged in the activities of the external world. When we attain the state of Sahaj Samadhi, this becomes possible.

Sahaj Samadhi

The ultimate goal of meditation is Sahaj Samadhi. This is a state in which we can naturally abide in the timeless state of being – in and through all our activities, at all times, whether we are awake, dreaming or in deep sleep, regardless of changes in mood, memory, weather, or surroundings. It becomes effortless for us to be in that state. We stabilize in that state forever. We remember who we truly are at all times, even while engaged in worldly activity. Just as a mirror serves as a medium to see ourselves, our body serves as a mirror to know our true nature. We witness the world of the senses only to know our sense of being. We neither become deluded by the experiences of the body nor by the world of the senses. We always have the conviction that whatever is happening is with the body and not with us. We are stabilized in the conviction that we are not the body; we are the sense of being, the sense of presence, which is eternal.

In this state, stabilized in the experience of the Self, we witness how our body functions in different situations. The qualities of the Self – such as love, joy, peace, compassion, patience, creativity and courage – are then expressed through our body. The body becomes the instrument for the highest expression of the Self.

DIRECT PATH — THE PATH OF LISTENING AND UNDERSTANDING

Whenever a seeker sets out on the path of truth, fundamental questions may arise in the mind such as "What is understanding truth? Can Self-realization be attained merely by listening?"

In the journey to realize our true nature, different paths have been propounded including chanting, penance and austerities, mystical practices, mantras, karma, religion, devotion, meditation, and knowledge. However, the path that is best is that of understanding.

Unless understanding is present when following these paths, they will not take the seeker to the supreme goal.

Hence, understanding has the highest importance in spirituality. A seeker who sets out on any path without understanding will not be able to reach the final goal. "Understanding" alone is complete in itself. Listening to the truth is enough to attain this understanding. Hence it has also been called the Path of Listening.* On the path of listening and understanding, the seeker can easily experience the answers to the questions: "Who am I? What is the essence of my being?"

Tejgyan can help you in understanding through listening. The Magic of Awakening retreat organized by Tejgyan Foundation is designed to help you progress further in this journey. You can get more information about this retreat in the Appendices.

COMPLETE MEDITATION

Meditation is complete only when Self-observation with awareness occurs. Complete Meditation brings together some of the meditations seen so far, but at the end of each meditation you turn within to see who is doing the meditation. When you turn within to ask who is meditating, the mind falls. The mind is master when consciousness goes to sleep. The mind becomes a servant when consciousness announces itself as the master, backed by the strength of Complete Meditation. What happens in Complete Meditation? The "experiencer" experiences the "experiencer" in and through every experience.

Begin this meditation by following the procedure given below. First read this procedure again and again to assimilate it fully in your mind.

1. Close your eyes and pray for good results with no expectation that anything particular should happen. Then sit in a meditation posture with a mudra.

2. Keeping the body steady, listen to all the sounds around you. Identify at least five different sounds. Don't be in a hurry. With a quiet mind, focus your attention on various sounds. Don't get stuck with a particular sound and only listen to that. Just identify each sound and move ahead.

3. If you hear the sound of a rotating fan, then there will be other subtle sounds within that sound too. Listen to them attentively. Various types of sounds can include conversations of people, clattering of vessels, children playing, horns, and sounds from different vehicles. There can be the sound of water flowing, the sound of something falling, the sound of somebody's footsteps, the sounds of television, music system or radio, the sound of birds singing, the sound of dogs barking

or fighting, or the sound of laughing or crying. When there are no sounds, then try to perceive the sound of silence. Feel the stillness.

4. Try to detect every type of sound around you. If you can hear the sound of aircraft in the sky, then notice the different sounds of different types of aircraft. Try to identify even the minutest of sounds. Listen to at least five different sounds – loud, medium or subtle.

5. After listening to these different sounds, ask yourself, "Am I these sounds?" The reply will come from within you: "I am not these sounds. I am the one who knows these sounds." Then turn within and see who this knower is, who is the ear of the ear. Tell yourself, "I am not the sound."

6. Now concentrate your attention on the atmosphere. Feel the atmosphere all around you and see whether the body feels light or heavy, whether the environment is hot or cold, dry or humid, whether there is a swift wind or a gentle breeze, fresh air or less air.

7. If you are able to feel the air, the heat, or the cold, then ask yourself, "Am I this atmosphere?" A reply will emerge: "No, I am not this atmosphere. I am the one who perceives or knows this atmosphere." Then tell yourself, "Turn around", and know the one who knows. Tell yourself, "I am not the atmosphere."

8. Now concentrate your attention on your body. If there is stiffness or pain in any part of the body, just know it experientially. Do not let the body move even a little.

9. Feel the parts of the whole body – where there is lightness or heaviness, where clothes touch, where air is felt, where itching or dryness occurs, where there is sweating, where there is a burning sensation. In this way, see all the subtle or gross sensations inside and outside the body.

10. Do not imagine anything; just feel what is happening in or on the body. Do not dismiss any of the feelings happening at present. Do not consider any feeling as good or bad; just feel it as it is. After witnessing all these sensations, after knowing what is happening in the whole body, ask yourself, "Am I these sensations?" The reply will arise: "No, I am not these sensations. I am the knower of these sensations." Then immediately turn around and shift to the knower, reach there. Tell yourself, "I am not these sensations."

11. Now focus your attention on your breathing. Just watch how your breathing is occurring. Feel through which nostril you are inhaling and through which nostril you are exhaling. When the breath is going inside, be aware of the breath going inside. When the breath is coming out, then be aware that the breath is coming out.

12. Feel the dashing of breath when the breath goes through your nose and dashes against the opening of the nostril. Feel whether the air that goes in and that which comes out is warm or not, know this as deeply as possible.

13. If your attention goes astray, bring it back to your breathing again. Perceive whether the breath went in silently or with a sound, and came out silently or with a sound. Note whether the breath is shallow, deep, or heavy. However your breath is, keep knowing it without labeling it.

14. Continue to observe whether the breath is coming out through the left nostril or the right nostril. In this way you are preparing for meditation and going towards Self Meditation (meditation on the Self). Ask yourself, "Am I this breath?" The reply will emerge: "No, I am not this breath. I am the knower of this breath." Now know this knower and tell yourself, "I am not the breath."

15. Now shift your attention from breathing and focus it on the thoughts that arise within. Watch the thoughts that are arising in your mind at this moment. After knowing one thought, know the next thought that arises. There is no need to pursue the previous thought. Just watch a thought and say, "Next."

    If you get a thought such as, "No thought is coming at all," then you have to understand that this is also a thought. After seeing it, say, "Next." As you go on watching thoughts, you will also feel the joy of detachment from thoughts. Watching all the thoughts that are arising in the mind, ask yourself, "Am I these thoughts?" The reply will appear: "No, I am not thoughts. I am the knower of thoughts." Now know that knower. Without moving the body, know the thoughts, and tell yourself, "I am not these thoughts."

16. Now focus your attention on your hands. Know how you are feeling in your hands. Take your attention also to your arms and experience how you are feeling there. See if you are able to feel the arms or not, or whether they feel heavy or light. Just know whatever you are feeling. Ask yourself, "Am I these hands or arms?" The reply will come: "No, I am not these hands or arms. I know these hands and arms." Immediately turn your attention back within and know the one who knows these hands and arms. If you are not the hands or arms, then who are you? Ask yourself this question. (Even if you are unable to know the knower, your true Self, continue the meditation without getting disappointed.)

17. Now take your attention to both your legs. See whether you are able to feel your legs, whether there is pressure on them or lightness in them. Without using a label of good or bad, ask yourself, "Am I these legs?" The reply will come: "No, I am the knower of these legs." Then know that knower. Tell yourself, "I am not the legs." If you are not the legs, then who are you?

Ask yourself this question.

18. Now, to help with the answer, take your attention to the back. See how your back feels. Just know how it is feeling from the shoulders to the waist, whether it is feeling light, heavy, painful, or if there is any pressure. Ask yourself, "Am I this back?" The reply will come: "No, I am the knower of this back." Shifting your focus within, know the knower, and tell yourself, "I am not this back."

19. Now bring your attention to your torso and the heart. Continue to know how the whole region feels. Ask yourself, "Am I the stomach, am I the heart, am I the neck, am I the shoulders? If I am not all of these, then who am I?" The answer comes: "I am the knower of all these parts." Immediately shift your attention and know this knower.

20. Now focus your attention on your face. If you are not other parts of your body, then feel your face. See whether you are able to feel your face, whether you feel lightness on the face or some sweat on the face. Know whether you feel pressure on the eyes or the eyes feel light. Then ask yourself, "Am I this face?" The reply will emerge: "No, I am the knower of this face." Shifting your focus, know the knower.

21. Tell yourself, "I am not this face, I am not this body, I am not the parts of this body, I am not the breath that is going through this body, I am not the thoughts, I am not the mind that is nothing but a bundle of thoughts. Then who am I? I am the knower of these. I have associated with this body to meditate on the Self, and to know the Self." As soon as you understand this, your attachment to the body will break. You will use your body, not vice versa.

22. After some time, while remaining in this state, open your eyes.

APPENDICES

Why Meditate?	Eagle Meditation	8
Demystifying Meditation	"I Don't Know" Meditation	16
Understanding True Meditation	Listening Meditation	21
Benefits of Meditation	Music Meditation	29
The Inward Journey	Mantra Meditation	38
The Daily Practice	Gratitude Meditation	45
The Preliminary Rituals	Reverse Words Meditation	53
	Walking Meditation	54
Attain Deeper Attunement	Number Meditation	63
Roadblocks in the Journey	"Attention on Attention" Meditation	72
Distractions in The Journey	Neutral Meditation	77
Obstacles During Meditation	A to Z Meditation	83
Stages in The Journey	Thought Numbering Meditation	94
External Training	Thought Watching Meditation	

Art of Witnessing	Thought Interval Meditation	103
	Breathing Meditation	110
	Breath Interval Meditation	112
Witness Your Thoughts	"How is my mind?" Meditation	122
Witness Your Emotions	Body Watching Meditation	127
The Ultimate Goal	Complete Meditation	135

* * *

You can mail your opinion or feedback on this book to:
books.feedback@tejgyan.org

APPENDIX - II

About Sirshree

Sirshree's spiritual quest, which began during his childhood, led him on a journey through various schools of philosophy and meditation practices. He studied a wide range of literature on mind science and spirituality. After a long period of deep contemplation on the truth of life, his quest culminated in attaining the ultimate truth.

Sirshree espouses, "All spiritual paths that lead to the truth begin differently but culminate at the same point – Understanding. This understanding is complete in itself. Listening to this understanding is enough to attain the Truth." Over the last two decades, he has dedicated his life to raise mass consciousness.

Sirshree has delivered more than 4000 discourses that throw light on this understanding. He has designed a system for wisdom, which makes it accessible to all. This system has inspired people from all walks of life to progress on their journey of the Truth. Thousands of seekers join in a virtual prayer for World Peace and Global Healing daily at 9:09 am and 9:09 pm.

About Tej Gyan Foundation

Tej Gyan Foundation is a non-profit organization founded on the teachings of Sirshree. The Foundation disseminates Tejgyan – the wisdom that guides one from self-development to Self-realization, leading towards Self-stabilization.

The Foundation's system for imparting wisdom has been assessed by international quality auditors and accredited with the ISO 9001:2015 certification. This wisdom has been presented in a simple, systematic, and practically applicable form that makes it accessible to people from all walks of life, regardless of religion, caste, social strata, country, or belief system.

The Foundation has centers in more than 400 cities and towns across India and other countries. The mission of Tej Gyan Foundation is to create a highly evolved society by leading seekers from negative thoughts to positive thoughts and further, from positive thoughts to Happy thoughts. A 'Happy thought' is the auspicious thought of being free from all thoughts, leading to the state of supreme bliss beyond thoughts.

If you seek such wisdom that leads you beyond mere knowledge, dissolves all problems, frees you from all limiting beliefs, reveals the true nature of divinity, and establishes you in the ultimate truth, then it is time to discover Tejgyan; it is time to rise above the mundane knowledge of words and experience Tejgyan!

The MahaAasmani Magic of Awakening Retreat

Self-development to Self-realization towards Self-stabilization

Do you wish to experience unconditional happiness that is not dependent on any reason? Happiness that is permanent and only increases with time? Do you wish to experience love, peace, self-belief, harmony in relationships, prosperity, and true contentment? Do you wish to progress in all facets of your life, viz. physical, mental, social, financial, and spiritual?

If you seek answers to these questions and are thirsty for the ultimate truth, then you are welcome to participate in the MahaAasmani Magic of Awakening retreat organized by Tej Gyan Foundation. This is the Foundation's flagship retreat based on the teachings of Sirshree.

The purpose of this retreat

The purpose of this retreat is that every human being should:

- Discover the answer to "Who am I" and "Why am I?" through direct experience and be established in ultimate bliss.

- Learn the art of living in the present, free from the burden of the past and the anxiety of the future.

- Acquire practical tools to help quieten the chattering mind and dissolve problems.

- Discover missing links in the practices of Meditation (Dhyana), Action (Karma), Wisdom (Gyana), and Devotion (Bhakti).

About Books by Sirshree

Sirshree's published work includes more than 150 book titles, some of which have been translated into more than 10 languages. His literature provides a profound reading on various topics of practical living and unravels the missing links in karma, wisdom, devotion, meditation, and consciousness.

His books have been published by leading publishing houses like Penguin, Hay House, Bloomsbury, Wisdom Tree, Jaico, etc. "The Source" book series, authored by Sirshree, has sold over 10 million copies. Various luminaries and celebrities like His Holiness the Dalai Lama, publishers Mr. Reid Tracy, Ms. Tami Simon and Yoga Master Dr. B. K. S. Iyengar have released Sirshree's books and lauded his work.

The Source
Attain Both, Inner Peace
and Worldly success

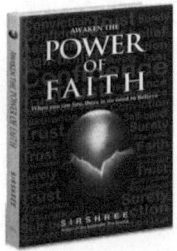

Awaken the Power of Faith
Discover the 7 Principles of the
Highest Power of the Universe

To order books authored by Sirshree, login to:
www.gethappythoughts.org
For further details, call: +91 9011013210

Tej Gyan Foundation – Contact details

Registered Office:
Happy Thoughts Building, Vikrant Complex, Near Tapovan Mandir, Pimpri, Pune 411017, INDIA. Contact: +91 20-27411240, +91 20-27412576

MaNaN Ashram:
Survey No. 43, Sanas Nagar, Nandoshi Gaon, Kirkatwadi Phata, Off Sinhagad Road, Taluka Haveli, Pune district - 411024, INDIA. Contact: +91 992100 8060.

WORLD PEACE PRAYER

Divine Light of Love, Bliss, and Peace is Showering;

The Golden Light of Higher Consciousness is Rising;

All negativity on Earth is Dissolving;

Everyone is in Peace and Blissfully Shining;

O God, Gratitude for Everything!

Members of Tej Gyan Foundation have been offering this impersonal mass prayer for many years. Those who are happy can offer this prayer. Those feeling low or suffering from illness can receive healing with this prayer.

If you are feeling troubled or sick, please sit to receive the healing effect of this prayer. Visualize that the divine white healing light is being showered on earth through the prayers of thousands and is also reaching you, bringing you peace and good health. You can dwell in this feeling for some time and then offer your gratitude to those offering the prayer.

A Humble Appeal

More than a million peace lovers pray for World Peace and Global Healing every morning and evening at 9:09. Also, a prayer (in Hindi) to elevate consciousness is webcast every day on YouTube at 3:30 pm and 9:00 pm IST. Please participate in this noble endeavor.

www.ingramcontent.com/pod-product-compliance
Lightning Source LLC
LaVergne TN
LVHW041844070526
838199LV00045BA/1426